# The Southeast

## GEORGIA • KENTUCKY • TENNESSEE

By
Thomas G. Aylesworth
Virginia L. Aylesworth

CHELSEA HOUSE PUBLISHERS
New York • Philadelphia

3   5   7   9   8   6   4


**Library of Congress Cataloging-in-Publication Data**

Aylesworth, Thomas G.
    The Southeast: Georgia, Kentucky, Tennessee
Thomas G. Aylesworth, Virginia L. Aylesworth.
        p. cm.—(Discovering America)
        Includes bibliographical references and index.
        ISBN 0-7910-3411-9.
                0-7910-3429-1 (pbk.)
        1. Southern States—Juvenile literature. 2. Georgia—Juvenile literature. 3. Kentucky—Juvenile
literature. 4. Tennessee—Juvenile literature. I. Aylesworth, Virginia L. II. Series: Aylesworth,
Thomas G. Discovering America.

F209.3.A953   1995                          94-42017
976.8—dc20                                   CIP
                                             AC

# CONTENTS

# TENNESSEE 63

# Georgia

The state seal of Georgia was adopted in 1798. It is circular, and in the center is an arch labeled "Constitution," supported by three columns labeled "Wisdom," "Justice," and "Moderation." In between the justice and moderation columns stands a man holding a drawn sword, representing the aid of the military in defending the constitution. Around the top of the circle is written "State of Georgia." At the bottom of the circle is 1776.

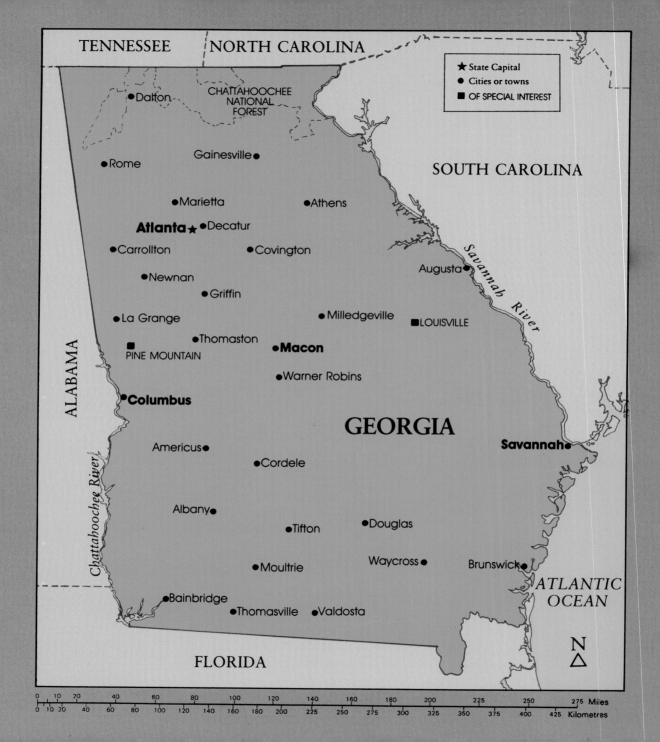

# GEORGIA

## At a Glance

**Capital:** Atlanta

**State Bird:** Brown Thrasher

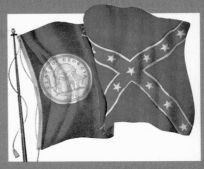

**State Flag**

**Major Crops:**

Peanuts, corn, soybeans, tobacco, wheat, cotton

**Major Industries:**

Manufacturing (textiles, pulp and paper products), forestry, agriculture

**State Flower:** Cherokee Rose

**Size:** 58,910 square miles (21st largest)
**Population:** 6,751,404 (11th largest)

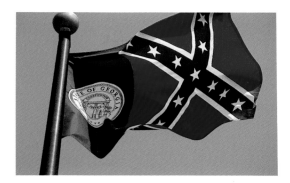

## State Flag

Georgia had several previous state flags—in 1799, 1861, 1879, and 1905—before the present state flag, designed by John Sammons Bell, was adopted in 1956. On the left, one-third of the flag is blue, bearing the state seal. The other two-thirds show the Confederate battle flag, with its red background and two blue diagonal lines containing 13 white stars representing the Confederate states.

## State Mottoes

*Agriculture and Commerce, 1776*
*Wisdom, Justice, Moderation*

The original motto carried the date 1799, which was the date of Georgia's admission to the Union. In 1914, it was changed to 1776, the date of national independence. The three words in the second motto refer to the virtues that should guide the three branches of the state government—legislative, judicial, and executive.

*The Okefenokee Swamp, a cypress-wooded wetland 45 miles long and 20 miles wide, is a place of eerie beauty.*

### State Capital

The first capital of the Georgia colony was Savannah. During the Revolutionary War, it was moved to Augusta, then Louisville, Milledgeville, and Macon. Finally, in 1868, it was moved to Atlanta.

### State Name and Nicknames

In 1732, King George II of England granted a charter to James Oglethorpe to found a colony in the New World. It was to be called Georgia, after the ruler, and it became the last of the 13 colonies.

Officially, Georgia has no nickname, but unofficially, it is commonly called the *Peach State* because of the economic importance of peaches. It is also a peanut-growing state and is occasionally referred to as the *Goober State*. Since it is one of the most economically important states in the country, it is sometimes called the *Empire State of the South* and the *Yankee-Land of the South*. Sometimes Georgia is called the *Cracker State* (after the old nickname for Georgia settlers who came from the mountains of Virginia and North Carolina) and the *Buzzard State* (since buzzards were once protected by law there).

### State Flower

The Cherokee rose, *Rosa sinica*, was named the state flower of Georgia in 1916. The Georgia Federation of Women's Clubs suggested the selection, and at the time it was believed that the flower was native to the area. Later it was found that it had come from China, had been introduced to England and brought to the New World in the late 1700s.

### State Wildflower

The azalea (family *Ericaceae*) was adopted as state wildflower in 1979.

### State Tree

*Quercus virginiana*, the live oak, which flourishes along the coast, was named the state tree in 1937.

### State Atlas

*The Atlas of Georgia* was adopted as the state atlas in 1985.

### State Fish

The largemouth bass (family *Centrarchidae*) was adopted as the state fish in 1970.

### State Bird

In 1935, the governor of Georgia named the brown thrasher, *Toxostoma rufum*, the state bird, but the legislature did not pass a law making this official until 1970.

### State Game Bird

The bobwhite quail, *Colinus virginianus*, was made the state game bird in 1970 because of the popularity of hunting in the state. Georgia is sometimes called the "Quail Capital of the World."

### State Fossil

The shark tooth, which is fairly common along the coast, became the state fossil in 1976.

**State Gem**

In 1976, quartz was chosen as the state gem.

**State Insect**

The honeybee, *Apis mellifera,* was named state insect in 1975.

**State Marine Mammal**

*Eubalaena glacialis*, the right whale, became the state marine mammal in 1985.

**State Mineral**

Staurolite became the state mineral in 1976.

**State Pledge of Allegiance**

The state pledge of allegiance to the Georgia flag is "I pledge allegiance to the Georgia flag and to the principles for which it stands: Wisdom, Justice, and Moderation."

**State Song**

The first state song, "Georgia," with music by Robert Loveman and words by Lollie Bell Wylie, was selected in 1922. This was later repealed. "Georgia On My Mind," with music by Hoagy Carmichael and words by Stuart Gorrell, was adopted as the state song in 1979.

**State Waltz**

"Our Georgia" was adopted as state waltz in 1951. It was composed in 1950 by James B. Burch.

**Population**

The population of Georgia in 1992 was 6,751,404, making it the 11th most populous state. There are 116.6 persons per square mile.

**Industries**

The principal industries in Georgia are forestry, agriculture, and the manufacture of textiles, transportation equipment, food, clothing, paper and wood products, and chemical products.

**Agriculture**

The chief crops of the state are peanuts, corn, peaches, soybeans, tobacco, oats, wheat, cotton, and cottonseed. Georgia is also a livestock state, and there are estimated to be almost 1.4 million cattle, 1.1 million hogs and pigs, and 8.8 million poultry on its farms. Pine and hardwood timber is harvested, and clay and crushed stone are important mineral products. Commercial fishing earned $23 million in 1992.

**Government**

The governor is elected to a four-year term, as are the lieutenant governor, attorney general, commissioner of agriculture, commissioner of labor, comptroller general, secretary of state, state school superintendent, and treasurer. The general assembly, which meets annually, consists of a 56-member senate and a 180-member house of representatives, all elected to two-year terms. One senator is elected from each of the 56 senatorial districts, and from one to four representatives are elected from the 154 representative districts. The most recent state constitution was adopted in 1982. In addition to its two U.S. senators, Georgia has ten representatives in the U.S. House of Representatives. The state has 12 votes in the electoral college.

**Sports**

Athletic contests of all kinds are held all over the state of Georgia. In 1983, the East Marietta National team of Marietta won the Little League World Series. On the collegiate level, the University of Georgia football team has won the Rose Bowl (1943), the Orange Bowl (1942, 1960), the Sugar Bowl (1947, 1981), and the Cotton Bowl (1967, 1984). Georgia Tech has won the Rose Bowl

*Lake Oconee, one of many man-made lakes in Georgia, provides a fine setting for sporting activities.*

(1929), the Orange Bowl (1940, 1948, 1952), the Sugar Bowl (1944, 1953, 1954, 1956), and the Cotton Bowl (1955).

On the professional level, the Atlanta Braves of the National League play baseball in the Atlanta-Fulton County Stadium, and the Atlanta Falcons of the National Football League share the same facility. The Atlanta Hawks of the National Basketball Association play in The Omni.

## Major Cities

*Albany* (population 78,122). This site was first inhabited by the Creek Indians who called it Skywater. It was laid out by Alexander Shotwell in 1836 and was named after the New York capital. Located in southwest Georgia at the head of the Flint River, it is the seat of Dougherty county and is a major industrial and commercial center. It is the trade center for this agricultural region specializing in cotton, corn, peanuts and tobacco.

*Atlanta, already one of the country's busiest convention cities, will host the 1996 Summer Olympic Games.*

*Places to visit in Albany:*
Albany Museum of Art, Wetherbee Planetarium and Space Museum, Thronateeska Heritage Foundation, Chehaw Wild Animal Park, and Lake Worth.

*Atlanta* (population 393,929). Originally, Atlanta was a Creek Indian settlement called Standing Peachtree. In 1813, a fort was built on the site. Founded in 1837, the capital of the state was only 27 years old when it was almost completely destroyed by Union troops after a 117-day siege. Today it is one of the most modern cities in the country, with some 1,770 manufacturers making 3,500 different products.

*Places to visit in Atlanta:*
State Capitol (1884-1889), Georgia State Museum of Science and Industry, A. G. Rhodes Memorial Hall (1903), Martin Luther King, Jr.,

National Historic Site, Robert W. Woodruff Arts Center, High Museum of Art, Swan House (1928), Tullie Smith House Restoration (1835), Walter McElreath Hall, Museum of the Jimmy Carter Library, Wren's Nest, Fox Theater (1929), Grant Park, Zoo Atlanta, Chastain Memorial Park Amphitheater, Fernbank Science Center, Atlanta State Farmers' Market, Six Flags Over Georgia, Stone Mountain Park, Yellow River Wildlife Game Ranch, and Fort McPherson.

*Columbus* (population 178,681). Founded in 1828, Columbus is at the navigable head of the Chattahoochee River in western Georgia. Creek Indians were the first people to live here and it soon became a border stronghold. In 1689 a Spanish fort was built here, called Fort Colon, and in 1826 these Indian lands were ceded to the state. Columbus served as a center of military operation in the Indian War of 1836, and in 1846 it was the point of departure for troops going to the Mexican War. The city supported the Confederate troops during the Civil War with shoes, caps, swords, pistols, and cannon. After the war, it became a great iron-working center and was second in the south in cotton manufacturing by World War II. Today it is still a charming town, but also a manufacturing center.

*Places to visit in Columbus:*
Fort Benning, National Infantry Museum, Columbus Museum, Rankin House (1850-1870), Walker-Peters-Langdon House (1828), Pemberton House, Columbus Iron Works Convention and Trade Center, Confederate Naval Museum, and Springer Opera House (1871).

*Macon* (population 107,365). Founded in 1823 as a trading post, it was later rebuilt as a fort. Over the years, Macon became a river landing for shipping, a cotton market, and a railroad center. During the Civil War, the city manufactured supplies, weapons, and ammunition. Today it remains a manufacturing center.

*Places to visit in Macon:*
Macon Museum of Arts and Sciences and Mark Smith Planetarium, City Hall (1836), Sidney Lanier Cottage (1840), Old Cannonball House and Macon Confederate Museum (1853), Hay House (1855), Grand Opera House (1884), and Ocmulgee National Monument.

*Savannah* (population 137,812). Founded in 1733, Savannah was planned by James Oglethorpe. By the time of the Revolutionary War it was a thriving port. After the war, the cultivation of tobacco began, and Eli Whitney's cotton gin was working at full speed. In 1819, the *Savannah*, the first steamer to cross the Atlantic, sailed for Liverpool, and the city became the leading port for shipping cotton, naval stores, and tobacco. Today, more than 1,000 historic buildings have been restored, and the city is also a manufacturing and shipping center.

*The Lockheed Aeronautical Systems Corporation has been in Marietta since 1951 and has delivered more than 3,000 airplanes.*

*Places to visit in Savannah:* City Hall (1905), Historic Savannah Waterfront Area, U.S. Customs House (1850), Factors Walk, Great Savannah Exposition, Grand Museum Hall, Trustees' Garden Site (1733), Pirate's House (1734), Christ Episcopal Church (1838), Telfair Mansion and Art Museum (1818), Owens-Thomas House (1817-1819), Davenport House (1815-1820), William Scarbrough House (1818), Juliette Gordon Low Birthplace (1818-1821), Andrew Low House (1848), Colonial Park Cemetery (1753), Georgia Historical Society, Green-Meldrim House, Congregation Mickve Israel, Ships of the Sea Maritime Museum, Laurel Grove Cemetery (South), Savannah Science Museum, and Wormsloe Plantation Historic Site.

## Places to Visit

The National Park Service maintains 11 areas in the state of Georgia: Andersonville National Historic Site, Appalachian National Scenic Trail, Kennesaw Mountain National Battlefield Park, Chickamauga and Chattanooga National Military Park, Fort Frederica National Monument, Fort Pulaski National Monument, Ocmulgee National Monument, Okefenokee National Wildlife Refuge, Cumberland Island National Seashore, Chattahoochee National Forest, and Oconee National Forest. In addition, there are 41 recreation areas.

**Albany**: Thronateeska Heritage Foundation. A complex of former railroad buildings housing exhibits on local and natural history.

**Athens**: Church-Waddell-Brumby House. A restoration of the oldest residence in Athens (1820).

**Augusta**: St. Paul's Episcopal Church. The church was built in 1750, near the site of a fort.

**Brunswick**: Mary Miller Doll Museum. More than 4,000 dolls, dollhouses, miniatures, boats, and toys are on exhibit.

**Calhoun**: New Echota State

Historic Site. The restorations of many homes and businesses of the early 1800s, when the town was the capital of the Cherokee Nation, include a supreme court building.

*Cartersville*: Etowah Indian Mounds and Archaeological Area. The remains of a

*On the property of Fickling house are over one-hundred thousand cherry blossom trees, which make Macon the cherry blossom capital of the world.*

thousand-year-old Indian settlement include six earthen pyramids.

*Chatsworth*: Vann House. This brick, three-story house, in modified Georgian style, was built in 1804 by James Vann, who was half Cherokee.

*Dahlonega*: Gold Miners' Camp. Visitors can pan for gold in this authentic mining setting.

*Darien*: Fort King George. This reconstruction of a 1721 fort, built by scouts from South Carolina, includes an Indian village.

*Eatonton*: Uncle Remus Museum. Made of two slave cabins, the log house displays shadow boxes illustrating several tales.

*Gainesville*: Green Street Historical District. Many houses, some dating back to the late nineteenth century, flank the tree-lined street.

*Helena*: Museum of the Hills. This is an authentic reconstruction of rural and village lifestyles in North Georgia at the turn of the century.

*La Grange*: Bellevue. Built from 1852 to 1853, this is a Greek Revival mansion.

*Lumpkin*: Bedingfield Inn. This stagecoach stop and doctor's residence was built in 1836.

*The Masters Golf Tournament in Augusta, played in the early spring, is one of the most prestigious tournaments on the PGA tour.*

*Marietta*: Big Shanty Museum. The famous Civil War steam railroad engine General is housed here.

*Pine Mountain*: Callaway Gardens. This site includes gardens, lakes, greenhouses, and recreation facilities.

*Rome*: Chieftains Museum. This eighteenth-century house was the home of prominent Cherokee leader

Major Ridge.

***St. Simons Island***: Christ Church, Frederica. Built in 1884, it is located on the site where John and Charles Wesley, the founders of the Methodist religion, had a congregation.

***Thomasville***: Pebble Hill Plantation. This historic plantation dates from the 1820s.

***Tifton***: Georgia Agrirama-Agriculture Heritage Center. Exhibits include working 19th-century farms, a school, and gristmill.

***Toccoa***: Traveler's Rest State Historic Site. This plantation house, built in 1825, became a stagecoach inn and post office.

***Valdosta***: The Crescent. A three-story colonial house that is named for its 15-column, crescent-shaped porch.

## Events

There are many events and organizations that schedule activities of various kinds in the state of Georgia. Here are some of them:

***Sports***: Albany Horse Show (Albany); Crackerland Tennis Tournament (Athens); Atlanta Hunt and Steeplechase (Atlanta); Atlanta Golf Classic (Atlanta); auto racing at Atlanta International Raceway (Atlanta); Masters Golf Tournament (Augusta); auto racing at Road Atlanta (Gainesville); Helen-to-Atlanta Canoe Classic (Helen); Balloon Races and Festival (Helen); BellSouth Atlanta Golf Classic (Marietta); Grand Prix International Regatta (Washington).

***Arts and Crafts***: Marigold Festival (Athens); Christmas Tour of Homes and Crafts Show (Athens); Georgia Mountain Fair (Hiawassee); Browns Crossing Craftsmen Fair (Milledgeville); Golden Isles Art Festival (St. Simons Island); Rose Festival (Thomasville).

***Music***: Atlanta Ballet (Atlanta); Atlanta Opera (Atlanta); Atlanta Symphony (Atlanta); jazz festivals (Atlanta); Augusta Symphony Orchestra (Augusta); Augusta Opera Association (Augusta); Beach Music Festival (Jekyll Island); Christmas Island (Jekyll Island); Savannah Symphony (Savannah).

***Entertainment***: Georgia Bluegrass Festival (Albany); National Pecan Festival (Albany); Andersonville Historic Fair (Andersonville); North Georgia Folk Festival (Athens); Atlanta Dogwood Festival (Atlanta); Georgia Renaissance Festival (Atlanta); Spring Fiesta (Brunswick); Appalachian Wagon Train (Chatsworth); Harvest Fair (Clayton); Watermelon Festival (Cordele); Prater's Mill Country Fair (Dalton); St. Patrick's Festival (Dublin); Cherry Blossom Festival (Macon); Georgia State Fair (Macon); Old Capital Celebration (Milledgeville); Farm-City Festival (Perry); Old Fashioned Christmas at the Crossroads (Perry); Heritage Holidays (Rome); Georgia Sea Island Festival (St. Simons Island); Georgia Week (Savannah); Night in Old Savannah (Savannah); Savannah Scottish Games (Savannah); Bite of the 'Boro and Blues Festival (Statesboro); "Tybee Jubilee" (Tybee Island); Okefenokee Spring Fling (Waycross); Forest Festival (Waycross); Okefenokee Heritage Festival (Waycross).

***Tours***: Historic Homes Tour (Athens); Fall Tour of Homes (Eatonton); Spring Tour of Homes (Madison); Home and Gardens Tour (St. Simons Island); Savannah Tour of Homes and Gardens (Savannah); Walking Tour of Old Savannah Gardens (Savannah).

***Theater***: Alliance Theatre Company (Atlanta); Theater of the Stars (Atlanta); Macon Little Theater (Macon).

The many rivers of the rugged Blue Ridge region are an important source of hydro-electric power for the state.

# The Land and the Climate

Georgia is a land of contrasts that include swamps and mountains, plains and canyons. It has one of the oldest planned cities in the country—Savannah—and one of the newest—Atlanta, which was rebuilt from the ashes of the Civil War.

Georgia has six main land regions: the Appalachian Plateau, the Appalachian Ridge and Valley Region, the Blue Ridge, the Piedmont, the Atlantic Coastal Plain, and the East Gulf Coastal Plain.

The Appalachian Plateau is in the northwest corner of the state. It is high country, with elevations of from 1,800 to 2,000 feet above sea level. There are narrow valleys and wooded hills here, but the thin, sandy soil makes it a poor farming area, although there are a few poultry farms and some commercial berry farms.

*Above:*
Georgia peaches, grown mainly in the southwest, are famous for their size and flavor and have become one of the state's trademarks.

Raising cotton, the most important natural fiber used to make clothing, is one of Georgia's leading industries. The state is one of the nation's top ten cotton producers. Large harvesters separate the cotton from its stem, or burr, and the ginning process cleans it by removing most of the seeds and other impurities from the cotton fibers.

*Above:*
The Okefenokee Swamp, in southeastern Georgia, extends into northeastern Florida. It is one of the country's largest swamps, comprising 700 square miles of tropical wilderness.

*Above right:*
Alligators, sandhill pipers, snowy egrets, and white ibises are among the many varieties of wildlife found in the swampy coastal areas of southern Georgia. Almost 300,000 acres of the Okefenokee serve as a national wildlife refuge, where these species and others are protected.

The Appalachian Ridge and Valley Region, in the northwest, skirts the Appalachian Plateau. Its broad valleys are good farming regions that specialize in cotton and poultry. Fruit, grain, vegetables, and beef cattle are raised here too. These valleys are separated by long ridges of higher ground.

The Blue Ridge lies in the northeastern corner of Georgia. Here the state's largest mountains range from 2,000 to nearly 5,000 feet—the highest being Brasstown Bald Mountain (4,784 feet). This is a region of hardwood and pine forests, and the rivers of the Blue Ridge are a major source of hydroelectric power.

The Piedmont is a region of small hills that cuts across the middle of Georgia. It is the state's most heavily populated area, which includes the cities of Atlanta, Augusta, Columbus, and Macon. On the southern edge of the Piedmont is what is called the Fall Line, where

the Piedmont rivers fall to the lower ground of the coastal plains, forming waterfalls and rapids. Farms in this well-watered area produce grains, nuts, and fruit.

The Atlantic Coastal Plain forms a large section of the southeastern part of Georgia—more than 25 percent of the state. It is a flat region with light, sandy soil that is ideal for growing peanuts, sweet potatoes, tobacco, and watermelons. It includes the eastern part of the Okefenokee Swamp.

The East Gulf Coastal Plain is in southwestern Georgia. It, too, is flat, but the land here is more fertile than that of the Atlantic Coastal Plain. The main crops here are corn, sorghum, sweet potatoes, vegetables, pecans, fruit, sugar cane, cotton, and peanuts. Beef cattle, hogs, and poultry are also raised here. The East Gulf Coastal Plain shares the Okefenokee Swamp with the Atlantic Coastal Plain.

The state has about 100 miles of coastline on the Atlantic Ocean: if all the bays, offshore islands, and river mouths are added, there are 2,344 miles of oceanfront land. The most important rivers in Georgia are the Altamaha, the Chattahoochee, the Flint, and the Savannah. Dams have formed lakes on several of Georgia's rivers, including Allatoona Lake, Clark Hill and Hartwell Reservoirs, and Lakes Lanier, Seminole, and Sinclair. Two of the most beautiful waterfalls in the state are Amicalola Falls (729 feet) on Amicalola Creek and Toccoa Falls (186 feet) on Toccoa Creek.

Georgia has an average annual temperature of 61.4 degrees Fahrenheit, and receives about 47 inches of precipitation yearly. Temperatures in summer range between 70 and 87 degrees F. and in winter from 37 to 52 degrees F.

Rafters enjoy riding the currents of the Chattahoochee, one of Georgia's largest rivers. It forms part of the Georgia-Alabama border, in the southwestern region of the state.

# The History

The original residents of what is now known as Georgia were the pre-historic Indians called the Mound Builders, whose culture has been studied through the tools and artifacts remaining in the large earthen mounds they constructed. By the time the first Europeans arrived in the sixteenth century, the land was occupied by the Creek Indians in the south and the Cherokee in the north.

It is probable that the Spanish explorer Hernando de Soto was the first white man to arrive in Georgia. In 1540 he passed through the area on his way west from Florida, during the expedition that would result in his discovery of the Mississippi River. The French came to Florida in 1564 and established a colony there, which angered King Philip II of Spain, who had claimed all of what is now the southeastern United States as Spanish territory. Therefore, the king dispatched Pedro Menéndez de Avilés to drive out the French. Once the French were defeated, the Spanish built forts along the Atlantic Coast, one of them on St. Catherines Island south of present–day Savannah.

Conflict between Spain and England marked the early years of Georgia's development, since the British also claimed the region and King Charles I had made it part of a colonial land grant in 1629. The English built a fort on the Altamaha River in 1721, but the expense of maintaining soldiers in the isolated post was so great that it was abandoned in 1727.

The British tried again in 1730, when some Englishmen planned to establish a new colony in the region, which they named Georgia for their king, George II. A leader of this group was James Oglethorpe, a member of the British Parliament, who wanted to populate the colony with debtors who had been imprisoned in England. This plan proved unworkable, and few released prisoners ever went to Georgia. Then George II granted a charter to an organization called Trustees for Establishing the Colony of Georgia in America. Even though Spain protested, Oglethorpe and his group of 120 settlers sailed from England on November 17, 1732, landing at Yamacraw Bluff, where Savannah is today, on February 12, 1733.

The king's charter for the colony of Georgia was for a period of 21 years; during that time more than 4,000 colonists arrived from England. The barrier islands off the coast of Georgia not only sheltered the fledgling colony, but also provided a bulwark against Spanish Florida. English forts were built in preparation for the long struggle for domination along the south Atlantic Coast. At the time, English ships were carrying on smuggling operations in these waters, many of them taking their goods to Spanish colonies in the West Indies. The combination of smuggling and controversy over the boundary between Florida and Georgia led to war between Spain and England in 1739. After a failed attempt to capture Florida, Oglethorpe stopped an invading Spanish army in the Battle of Bloody Marsh on St. Simons Island in 1742. This ended the fighting in colonial America, although the war between Spain and England continued in Europe.

St. Simons Island was the site of the Battle of Bloody Marsh, in which Georgia's founder, James Edward Oglethorpe, defeated a landing force of Spanish invaders in 1742. Oglethorpe was originally commissioned to colonize the area for England in an effort to shield South Carolina from possible attack by the Spanish, in Florida, and the French, in Louisiana.

Meanwhile, the Colony's trustees were bringing in English artisans to establish strong settlements in what would become Savannah, Brunswick, and Darien—where Scottish Highlanders introduced golf to the New World. Under Oglethorpe's supervision, peace was made with the Cherokee Indians, which enabled the colonists to follow the rivers that flowed into their settlements along the coast, and to found such inland communities as Augusta.

The trustees of Georgia gave up their 21-year charter in 1752, and King George II made the colony a royal province two years later. Its farms and communities developed peacefully for several decades. But then a desire for independence spread to Georgia, and many residents celebrated the beginning of the Revolutionary War in 1775. The Georgia patriots seized power, and James Wright, the royal governor, was forced to flee.

In March 1776, a British warship tried to seize 11 colonial boats loaded with rice in Savannah Harbor, and fierce fighting broke out between the Royal Navy and the patriots. Only two of the rice boats were lost to the British. In 1778 Georgia became a major battleground when British troops captured the coastal city of Savannah. With the help of French naval forces, an American army laid siege to the town, then attacked it three weeks later. The attack was a failure, and more than 1,000 colonists and Frenchmen were killed. By the end of 1779, the British were in control of the entire colony, except for Wilkes County, where the city of Washington now stands. Not until 1782 were the British driven from Georgia.

The Revolutionary War ended the following year, and Georgia became the fourth state to ratify the new Constitution in 1788. In 1793, near Savannah, Eli Whitney invented the cotton gin, which separated seeds from fiber, and Georgia became a major cotton-growing state as a result of the enormous saving in work time. The South was on its way to a single-crop economy.

The state of Georgia extended its western border to the Mississippi River, but the manipulations of land speculators in the legislature put much of what is now Mississippi and Alabama up for sale as the Yazoo Tract at 1½ cents an acre. This became known as the Yazoo Fraud (named for the Yazoo River, which ran through part of the land). Although the sale was repudiated by a later legislature and declared unconstitutional by the Supreme Court, the lands were gone forever and Georgia no longer reaches from the Mississippi to the Atlantic.

Georgia fared worse in the Civil War than some of the other Confederate States. Between the Revolution and the Civil War the state had based its cotton industry on slave labor. In 1860, when Lincoln was elected President and the future of slavery was called into even greater question in the North, Georgia was one of the first southern states to secede from the Union (in January, 1861). Early in the War, the Union Navy raided the Georgia coast and closed Savannah, its chief port. The first great battle in Georgia—Chickamauga—was won by the Confederates in 1863, but the following year General William Tecumseh Sherman began his March to the Sea. His Union soldiers advanced from Chattanooga, Tennessee, to Atlanta. The march began

These two cycloramas depict the Battle of Atlanta, during the summer-long campaign of 1864. The Confederate defenders, under the command of General J. B. Hood, sustained heavy casualties but held the city until September 1, when they were forced to evacuate it. On September 2 General Sherman and his men occupied Atlanta, which they destroyed two months later.

General William Tecumseh Sherman invaded Georgia in May 1864 with 98,000 Union soldiers. After capturing Atlanta and burning it almost to the ground, he headed east on his famous "March to the Sea." The capture of the port of Savannah in December dealt a powerful blow to the Confederacy, and Sherman's subsequent sweep through the Carolinas continued the destruction. The general's prime objective was to break the South's will to continue the war.

A view of the ruins of Atlanta after its capture by General Sherman's Union troops. Sherman's forces destroyed some $100,000,000 worth of property in Georgia after they burned Atlanta in November 1864.

in May 1864; Sherman captured the Georgia capital in September and burned it almost to the ground. He then marched across Georgia with little opposition, destroying about $100 million worth of property on his way to Savannah. The Union troops cut a path some 60 miles wide, destroying all factories, mills, public buildings, and railroads. They looted the countryside and stole food, livestock, and other property from farmers and city dwellers alike.

After the Civil War, the Union Army occupied Georgia during the years known as Reconstruction. The state was not readmitted to the Union until 1868, and it was promptly expelled (1869) for its refusal to ratify the Fifteenth Amendment to the Constitution, which gave all citizens of the United States the right to vote, regardless of race. Georgia finally ratified the amendment in 1870 and was then readmitted to the Union.

During the 1870s, Georgia began to increase its trade and manufacturing activities. The railroads were rebuilt, banks grew, and cities became more populous. There was money available for schools, social services, and farm loans. After the turn of the century, farmers became less dependent on cotton and began to raise more corn, fruit, livestock, and tobacco. During World War I, factory and farm production made significant gains, and some 103,500 Georgians served in the armed forces. The state's mineral resources, including granite, clay, marble and bauxite, were quarried and mined on a larger scale, and forest products added to the state's prosperity.

Governor Thomas W. Hardwick appointed the United States's first woman senator in 1922. She was Rebecca L. Felton, named to replace Senator Thomas E. Watson after his death in office. However, she served only a single day while the Senate was in session. After a long Congressional recess, she was replaced by Walter F. George, who had been elected to complete Watson's term.

During the 1920s, boll weevils destroyed much of Georgia's cotton crop, and many farmers went bankrupt even before the Great Depression of the 1930s. Then factories closed down and more farmers lost their land in bank failures and foreclosures. Federal programs assisted the recovery process, and when the United States entered World War II, factories and farms made dramatic comebacks. Army camps and defense factories began to spring up, and some 324,000 people from Georgia served in the armed forces.

After the war, Georgia spent considerable money and effort improving the educational system, hospitals, and roads. The Atlanta-born

Savannah, built on the site of the state's first white settlement, founded in 1733, is a busy port and commercial center.

minister, Martin Luther King, Jr., worked to join black Georgians together in peaceful protests, marches, sit-ins, and boycotts for equal rights. In 1961, a federal court ordered the University of Georgia to admit black students and other Georgia schools and colleges slowly followed their lead.

Georgia's economy continues to grow. Atlanta has become the most important business community in the Southeast, with more national manufacturing and commercial concerns than any other Southern city. Tourism is one of Georgia's major industries. Vacationers spent $10.4 billion in Georgia in 1991.

The University of Georgia, in Athens, is one of the most popular state-supported institutions of higher learning in Georgia. It was founded in 1785.

# Education

State-supported schools opened in Georgia in 1872. In 1785, the University of Georgia in Athens became the first state-chartered university in the nation. In 1902, Martha McChesney Berry built a small schoolhouse to teach poor mountain children. Approximately 2,000 students still use the Berry College's campus. The state now has some 27 institutions of higher education and more than 2,000 public elementary and secondary schools.

# The People

Approximately 17 percent of the population was born in the United States. About 65 percent of Georgians live in metropolitan areas. Except for a relatively small number of people from Canada and Europe, almost all Georgians were born in the United States. The largest religious body is the Baptist church, followed by Episcopalians, Methodists, Presbyterians, Roman Catholics, and the Disciples of Christ.

**Famous People**

Many famous people were born in the state of Georgia. Here are a few:

**Conrad Aiken** 1889-1973, Savannah. Pulitzer Prize-winning poet: *The Human Heart*

**James Bowie** 1796-1836, Burke County. Hero of the Texas Revolution

**Jim Brown** b.1936, St. Simons Island. Hall of Fame football player and actor

**Erskine Caldwell** 1903-1987, White Oak. Novelist: *Tobacco Road, God's Little Acre*

**James Earl Carter** b.1924, Plains. Thirty-ninth President of the United States

**Ray Charles** b.1930, Albany. Jazz, soul, and pop singer

**Lucius Clay** 1897-1978, Marietta. Army general and military governor of the U.S. zone of Germany (1947)

**Ty Cobb** 1886-1961, Narrows. Hall of Fame baseball player

**Ossie Davis** b.1917, Cogdell. Stage and film actor and director

**James Dickey** b.1923, Atlanta. Poet and novelist: *Buckdancer's Choice, Deliverance*

**Walt Frazier** b.1945, Atlanta. Hall of Fame basketball player

**John C. Fremont** 1813-1890, Savannah. Mapper of the Oregon Trail

*Jimmy Carter, once governor of Georgia, returned to his home state after his presidency.*

**Oliver Hardy** 1892-1957, Harlem. Half of the Laurel and Hardy comedy film team

**Joel Chandler Harris** 1848-1908, Putnam County. Short story writer: *Uncle Remus, His Songs and His Sayings, Uncle Remus and Br'er Rabbit*

**Fletcher Henderson** 1898-1952, Cuthbert. Jazz band leader

**Courtney Hodges** 1887-1966, Perry. World War II general

**Larry Holmes** b.1949, Cuthbert. Heavyweight boxing champion

**Jasper Johns** b.1930, Augusta. Pop artist

**Bobby Jones** 1902-1971, Atlanta. Championship golfer

**Vernon Jordan** b.1935, Atlanta. Civil rights leader

**Stacy Keach** b.1941, Savannah. Stage and film actor

**Martin Luther King, Jr.** 1929-1968, Atlanta. Nobel Peace

Prize-winning civil rights leader

**Gladys Knight** b.1944, Atlanta. Soul singer

**Sidney Lanier** 1842-1881, Macon. Poet: *The Song of the Chattahoochee, The Marshes of Glynn*

**Carson McCullers** 1917-1967, Columbus. Novelist: *The Heart Is a Lonely Hunter, A*

*Martin Luther King, Jr., the major figure in the black civil rights movement of the 1960's, delivered his most famous speech, "I Have a Dream," during the March on Washington in 1963.*

*Member of the Wedding*

**Johnny Mercer** 1909-1976, Savannah. Pop singer and lyricist

**Margaret Mitchell** 1900-1949, Atlanta. Novelist: *Gone With the Wind*

**Elijah Muhammad** 1897-1975, near Sandersville. Leader of the Nation of Islam

**Flannery O'Connor** 1925-1964, Savannah. Short story writer and novelist: *Wise Blood, The Violent Bear It Away*

**George Foster Peabody** 1852-1938, Columbus. Banker and philanthropist

**Ma Rainey** 1886-1939, Columbus. Blues singer

**Otis Redding** 1941-1967, Macon. Rhythm-and-blues singer

**Jerry Reed** b.1937, Atlanta. Country-rock singer

**Burt Reynolds** b.1936, Waycross. Film actor

**Little Richard** b.1932, Macon. Rock-and-roll singer

**Jackie Robinson** 1919-1972,

*In 1947, Jackie Robinson broke Major League baseball's color barrier. Hired by Branch Rickey, president of the Brooklyn Dodgers, he became the first black to play in the big leagues.*

Cairo. Hall of Fame baseball player

**Ruth Carter Stapleton** b.1930, Plains. Evangelist

**Alice Walker** b. 1944, Eatonton. Author of *The Color Purple*

**Herschel Walker** b. 1962, Wrightsville. Heisman Trophy-winning running back

**Wyomia Tyus** b.1945, Griffin. Olympic gold medal sprinter

**Joseph Wheeler** 1836-1906, Augusta. Confederate general

**Walter F. White** 1893-1955, Atlanta. Civil rights leader

**Jane Withers** b.1926, Atlanta. Child film star

**Joanne Woodward** b.1930, Thomasville. Academy Award-winning actress: *The Three Faces of Eve, Rachel, Rachel*

**Colleges and Universities**

There are many colleges and universities in Georgia. Here are the most prominent, with their locations, dates of founding, and enrollments.

*Albany State College,* Albany, 1903, 3,106

*Augusta College,* Augusta, 1925, 5,579

*Brenau University,* Gainesville, 1878, 1,987

*Clark Atlanta University,* Atlanta, 1869, 4,480

*Columbus College,* Columbus, 1958, 5,009

*Emory University,* Atlanta, 1836, 9,958

*Fort Valley State College,* Fort Valley, 1895, 2,368

*Georgia College,* Milledgeville, 1889, 5,501

*Georgia Institute of Technology,* Atlanta, 1885, 12,891

*Georgia Southern University,* Statesboro, 1906, 13,411

*Georgia State University,* Atlanta, 1913, 24,101

*Mercer University,* Macon, 1833, 6,348

*Morehouse College,* Atlanta, 1867, 2,990

*North Georgia College,* Dahlonega, 1873, 2,794

*Oglethorpe University,* Atlanta, 1835, 1,195

*Savannah College of Art and Design,* Savannah, 1978, 2,330

*Savannah State College,* Savannah, 1890, 3,100

*Spelman College,* Atlanta, 1881, 2,026

*University of Georgia,* Athens, 1785, 28,493

*Valdosta State College,* Valdosta, 1906, 7,898

*West Georgia College,* Carrollton, 1933, 7,717

**Where To Get More Information**

Chamber of Commerce
235 International Blvd.
Atlanta, GA 30303
or call, 1-800-VISITGA

# Kentucky

The state seal of Kentucky is circular in shape. In the center are two men shaking hands—one in a frontiersman's outfit and the other in a frock coat. Above the figures is "United We Stand," and below them is "Divided We Fall." Around the circle is written "Commonwealth of Kentucky." The seal was adopted in 1792.

# KENTUCKY
## At a Glance

**State Flag**

**Capital:** Frankfort

**State Flower:**
Goldenrod

**Major Crops:**
Tobacco, soybeans,
corn, wheat

**Major Industries:**

Manufacturing (machinery, transportation equipment, chemicals, tobacco products), coal mining, construction, agriculture, livestock

★ State Capital
● Cities or towns
■ OF SPECIAL INTEREST

ILLINOIS

Wabash R

Mississippi River

Ohio River

MISSOURI

Paducah

N

0   10   20        40        60        80        100 M

0  10  20     40     60     80    100   120   140   160  Kil

**State Bird:** Kentucky Cardinal
**State Motto:** United We Stand, Divided We Fall
**State Tree:** Kentucky Coffee Tree
**Nickname:** Bluegrass State
**State Song:** "My Old Kentucky Home"

**Size:** 40,410 square miles (37th largest)
**Population:** 3,754,715 (24th largest)

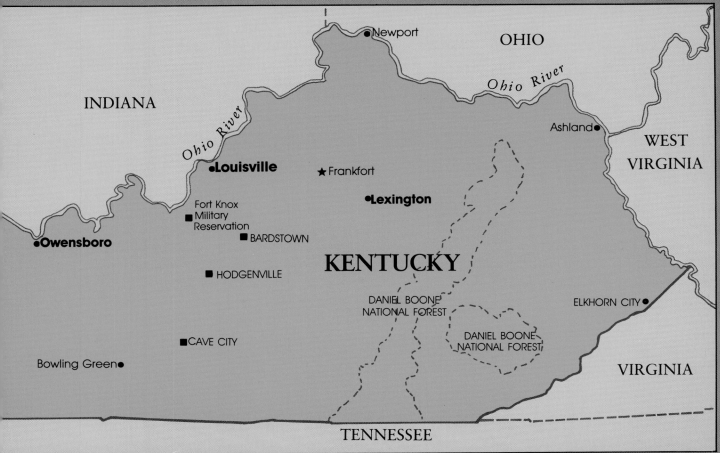

### State Flag
The state flag of Kentucky is navy blue, with the state seal in the center. Under the seal are two branches of goldenrod in bloom.

### State Motto
*United We Stand,*
*Divided We Fall*
This is an adaptation of a quotation from John Dickinson's "Liberty Song of 1768": "By uniting we stand; by dividing we fall."

*The Cumberland Gap, a natural pass through the Cumberland Mountains, was discovered in 1750.*

## State Name and Nicknames

The name "Kentucky" is thought to come from the Wyandot Indian word Kem-tah-teh, or "land of tomorrow."

The most common nickname for the commonwealth of Kentucky is the *Bluegrass State*, because of the dominant type of grass in the region. It is sometimes called the *Hemp State* and *Tobacco State* because of the former importance of these products to the economic history of the state. Finally, it is occasionally called the *Dark and Bloody Ground*, a term that Daniel Boone heard from an Indian chief to describe the many battles between settlers and Indians that had been fought there.

## State Flower

In 1926, the goldenrod, *Solidago juncea*, also called the yellow-top or flower-of-gold, was adopted as state flower.

## State Capital

Lexington was the state capital in 1792, but later that year it was decided to name Frankfort as the capital.

## State Tree

*Gymnocladus dioicus*, the coffee tree, was made the state tree in 1976.

## State Bird

Commonly called the Kentucky cardinal, *Cardinalis cardinalis* was adopted as the state bird in 1926.

## State Language

English was named the official language in 1984.

## State Shakespearean Festival

In 1984, Shakespeare in Central Park of Louisville was adopted as State Shakespearean Festival.

## State Wild Animal Game Species

*Sciurus carolinensis*, the gray squirrel, was adopted as state wild animal game species in 1968.

## State Tug-of-War Championship

The Nelson County Fair Tug-of-War Championship Contest was named in 1984.

## State Song

Stephen Foster's "My Old Kentucky Home" was chosen as state song in 1928.

## Population

The population of Kentucky in 1992 was 3,754,715, making it the 24th most populous state. There are 94.5 persons per square mile.

## Industries

The principal industries of the state of Kentucky are coal mining, construction, agriculture, and the manufacture of nonelectric machinery, food products, electric and electronic products, apparel, and primary metals.

## Agriculture

The chief crops of the state are tobacco, soybeans, corn, and wheat. Kentucky is also a livestock state, and there are estimated to be some 2.5 million cattle, 920,000 hogs and pigs, 35,000 sheep, and 2.2 million chickens on its farms.

## Government

The governor and lieutenant governor are elected to four-year terms, as are the attorney general, auditor of public accounts, commissioners of agriculture, labor, and statistics, secretary of state, superintendent of public instruction, and treasurer. The general assembly, which meets in even-numbered years, consists of a 38-member senate and a 100-member house of representatives. The senators serve four-year terms, and the representatives serve two-year terms. They are elected in senate and house districts. The most recent state constitution was adopted in 1891. In addition to its two U.S. senators, Kentucky has six representatives in the U.S.

*Lake Cumberland, covering over 50,000 acres, is one of Kentucky's major recreational areas. A 3,000-acre state park is situated on its shoreline.*

*The Federal Hill mansion near Bardstown, built in the Georgian style around 1795, inspired Stephen Foster to write one of his most famous songs, "My Old Kentucky Home."*

House of Representatives. The state has eight votes in the electoral college.

## Sports

Many sporting events on the collegiate and secondary school level are held all over the state. Kentucky is one of the premier basketball states. On the collegiate level, the NCAA national basketball championship has been won by the University of Kentucky (1948, 1949, 1951, 1958, 1978) and the University of Louisville (1980, 1986). The National Invitational Tournament has been won by the University of Kentucky (1946, 1976) and the University of Louisville (1956). In football, the University of Kentucky won the Cotton Bowl in 1952 and the Sugar Bowl in 1951.

## Major Cities

*Bowling Green* (population 40,688). Founded in 1780 by settlers from Virginia, it is named after the green on which lawyers and court officials played bowls during the court recess. Located in southwest Kentucky, it is the seat of Warren County. It is a center of manufacturing and its major agricultural products are corn, tobacco, and strawberries, and it produces grain, livestock, horses and poultry.

*Places to visit in Bowling Green:* Western Kentucky University, Mammoth Cave National Park.

*Frankfort* (population 26,535). Founded in 1786, Frankfort was named the state capital in 1792 as a compromise for those who supported Louisville and Lexington. It was briefly held by the Confederates during the Civil War. The Kentucky

*The Basilica of the Assumption, in Covington, modeled on the Cathedral of Notre Dame in Paris, was completed in 1901. It has the largest stained-glass window in the world.*

River meanders through the city, which lies in the center of rich farmland.

*Places to visit in Frankfort:*
State Capitol (1910), Kentucky's Floral Clock, Governor's Mansion (1914), Old State Capitol (1827-1830), Old Governor's Mansion (1798), Daniel Boone's Grave, Kentucky Military History Museum, Liberty Hall (1796-1801), and Orlando Brown House (1835).

*Lexington* (population 225,366). Founded in 1779, Lexington was settled by an exploring party who gave the site its name in 1775, when they heard about the Battle of Lexington, which started the Revolutionary War. The city was established four years later. It soon became a center for barter and later cashed in on its tobacco crop. Pioneers from Virginia and Maryland brought their best horses here; this is the origin of the thoroughbred race horses of the Bluegrass Country. Today, it is a wealthy city, renowned for its old homes and horse farms, and as an

*The 1,032-acre Kentucky Horse Park in Lexington is home to more than 32 breeds of horses and is host to 50 special events a year. Visitors can tour the farm as well as the museum and other exhibits.*

educational and cultural center.

*Places to visit in Lexington:*
Ashland (1806), Hunt-Morgan House (1814), Mary Todd Lincoln House, Headley-Whitney Museum, Guild Gallery, Opera House (1886), Lexington Cemetery, Victorian Square, Kentucky Horse Park, American Saddle Horse Museum, horse farms, and Chaumiere du Prairie.

*Louisville* (population 269,555). Founded in 1778, it

has always been a mixture of southern graces and a midwestern pace. It was explored, settled, and developed by Spanish, English, French, Scottish, Irish, and Germans. George Rogers Clark established the first real settlement as a base for military operations against the British. Named after King Louis XVI of France, today the city is a business and industrial

*The Kentucky Center for the Arts is the cultural center of the state. It boasts three stages and a distinguished sculpture collection.*

center. It is best known for its patronage of the arts and the annual Kentucky Derby horse race.

Places to visit in Louisville:
Zachary Taylor National Cemetery, Cave Hill Cemetery, Jefferson County Courthouse (1837), Water Tower, Museum of History and Science, Brennan House (1868), Farmington (1810), Locust Grove (1790), Thomas Edison House, Colonel Harland Sanders Museum, Old Louisville, Butchertown, Cherokee Triangle, Portland, J. B. Speed Art Museum, Rauch Memorial Planetarium, Churchill Downs, Kentucky Derby Museum, Kentucky Center for the Arts, Otter Creek State Park, Louisville Zoological Gardens, and Kentucky Botanical Gardens.

*Owensboro* (population 53,579). Originally settled in 1800, this site was known as Yellow Banks because of the deep yellow color of the soil. It became the county seat as Rossborough, named after David Ross, a large property owner. It was incorporated in 1817 and in 1836 was renamed Owensboro and chartered as a city. Located in northwest Kentucky on the Ohio River, this is a farming, dairying, and grazing region. Its products include oil, gas, coal, timber, tobacco, and whiskey.

Places to visit in Owensboro:
Kentucky Wesleyar and Brescia Colleges, Owensboro Museum of Fine Art, and Owensboro Area Museum

**Places to Visit**

The National Park Service maintains five areas in the state of Kentucky: Mammoth Cave National Park, Abraham Lincoln Birthplace National Historic Site, part of Breaks Interstate Park, part of Cumberland Gap National Historical Park, and Daniel Boone National Forest. In addition, there are 34 state recreation areas.

*Ashland*: Jesse Stuart's W-Hollow Nature Preserve. This

includes 715 acres of land where the noted author lived.

**Bardstown**: My Old Kentucky Home State Park. The park features a stately home, built in 1795, that belonged to a cousin of composer Stephen Foster, who often visited there.

**Bowling Green**: Riverview. Built in 1857, this is a mansion in Italian-villa style.

**Carrollton**: Historic District. A self-guided tour may be taken through the buildings.

**Cave City**: Crystal Onyx Cave and Campground Park. The cave tour also includes a prehistoric Indian burial ground dating from 680 B.C.

**Covington**: Basilica of the Assumption. Built in 1901, it is patterned after the Cathedral of Notre Dame and the Abbey of St. Denis in France.

**Crab Orchard**: William Whitley State House Historic Site. Built from 1785 to 1792, this is the oldest brick house west of the Alleghenies.

**Danville**: Constitution Square State Historic Site. This is an authentic reproduction of Kentucky's first courthouse square.

**Elizabethtown**: Brown-Pusey Community House. Built in 1825, this was once a stagecoach inn.

**Fort Knox**: Patton Museum of Cavalry and Armor. Weapons, armor, art, and uniforms are displayed here.

**Georgetown**: Scott County Courthouse. Built in 1877, it is a part of the historic business district.

**Gilbertsville**: Kentucky Dam. This is the largest dam in the Tennessee Valley Authority system.

**Harrodsburg**: Morgan Row. These are the oldest standing row houses west of the Alleghenies. They date from 1807 to 1845.

**Hodgenville**: Lincoln's Boyhood Home. A replica of the log cabin where Abraham Lincoln was born.

**Maysville**: Old Washington. Restored buildings, some dating back to the late 1700s, include an inn, a fort, and a trading post.

**Murray**: National Museum of the Boy Scouts of America. This museum houses scouting memorabilia and 53 original paintings by Norman Rockwell.

*Abraham Lincoln moved to this log cabin just outside of Hodgenville when he was two years old. The one-room cabin thought to have been his birthplace is also displayed in Hodgenville.*

*Owensboro*: Owensboro Museum of Fine Art. On display is a collection of American, French, and English art from the sixteenth to twentieth centuries.

*Paris*: Duncan Tavern Historic Shrine. The Duncan Tavern (1788) and the Anne Duncan House (1800), of log construction, have been restored.

*Park City*: Kentucky Diamond Caverns. Guided tours include views of some of the world's largest stalactites and stalagmites.

*Richmond*: Courthouse. Located in the downtown historic district, the building served as a hospital during the Civil War.

*South Union*: South Union Shaker Museum. Shaker crafts, furniture, textiles, and tools are exhibited in a building created by members of this 19th-century religious sect.

*Winchester*: Old Stone Church. This is the oldest active church west of the Alleghenies.

## Events

There are many events and organizations that schedule activities of various kinds in the state of Kentucky. Here

are some of them.

*Sports*: Tri-State Fair and Regatta (Ashland); Jim Beam Stakes Race at Turfway Park Race Track (Florence); Mason-Dixon Steeplechase, adjacent to Turfway Park Race Track (Florence); horse racing at Turfway Park Race Track (Florence); Jaycees Horse Show (Hazard); horse racing at Riverside Downs (Henderson); horse racing at James C. Ellis Park (Henderson); Blue Grass Stakes at Keeneland Race Course (Lexington); High Hope

Steeplechase at Kentucky Horse Park (Lexington); Rolex-Kentucky Event and Trade Fair at Kentucky Horse Park (Lexington); Junior League Horse Show (Lexington); Grand Circuit Meet at The Red Mile Track (Lexington); thoroughbred racing at Keeneland Race Course (Lexington); harness racing at The Red Mile (Lexington); Oxmoor Steeplechase (Louisville); horse racing at Churchill Downs including the annual Kentucky Derby (Louisville); horse racing at

*The annual Kentucky Derby, run at Churchill Downs in Louisville, is considered by many enthusiasts to be the premier thoroughbred racing event of the year.*

Louisville Downs (Louisville); Sternwheeler Annual Regatta (Maysville); National Coon Hunters Meeting and Hunt (Paducah).

**Arts and Crafts**: Kentucky Guild of Artists and Craftsmen's Fair (Berea); Berea Crafts Fair (Berea); Carousel of Arts (Henderson); Founder's Day (Hodgenville); St. James Court Art Fair (Louisville); Jackson Purchase Arts and Crafts Festival (Murray); Dogwood Trail Celebration (Paducah).

**Music**: "The Stephen Foster Story" (Bardstown); Music Festival (Berea); Capital Expo Festival (Frankfort); Festival of the Bluegrass (Lexington); Lexington Philharmonic (Lexington); Louisville Ballet (Louisville); Louisville Orchestra (Louisville); Kentucky Opera Association (Louisville); Bluegrass Music Festival of the United States (Louisville); Renfro Valley Barn Dance and Jamboree (Mount Vernon); Owensboro Symphony (Owensboro); Bluegrass with Class Festival (Owensboro).

**Entertainment**: Daniel Boone Festival (Barbourville); Bluegrass Festival (Berea); Kentucky Scottish Weekend (Carrollton); Nibroc Festival (Corbin); Mayfest (Covington); Hardin County Fair (Elizabethtown); Kentucky Heartland Festival (Elizabethtown); Armored Vehicle Presentation (Fort Knox); International Banana Festival (Fulton); Highland Games and Gathering of Scottish Clans (Glasgow); Pioneer Days Festival (Harrodsburg); Black Gold Festival (Hazard); Henderson County Fair (Henderson); LaRue County Fair (Hodgenville); Lincoln Day Celebration (Hodgenville); Little River Days (Hopkinsville); Western Kentucky State Fair (Hopkinsville); Egyptian Event (Lexington); Kentucky Derby Festival (Louisville); Kentucky State Fair and Horse Show (Louisville); Corn Island Storytelling Festival (Louisville); Christmas in the City (Louisville); Heritage Weekends (Louisville); Hopkins County Fair (Madisonville); Harvest Festival (Maysville); County Court Day (Maysville); Appalachian Celebration (Morehead); Kentucky Harvest and Hardwood Festival (Morehead); Calloway County Fair (Murray); International Bar-b-que Festival (Owensboro); Daviess County Fair (Owensboro); Kiwanis West Kentucky-McCracken County Fair (Paducah); Central Kentucky Steam and Gas Engine Show (Paris); Bourbon County Fair (Paris); Hillbilly Days Spring Festival (Pikeville); Mountain Laurel Festival (Pineville); Kentucky Highlands Folk Festival (Prestonburg); Kentucky Apple Festival (Prestonburg); Madison County Fair and Horse Show (Richmond); Shaker Festival (South Union); Tobacco Festival (South Union); Daniel Boone Pioneer Festival (Winchester).

**Theater**: Pioneer Playhouse (Danville); "The Legend of Daniel Boone" (Harrodsburg); "Lincoln" (Harrodsburg); Horse Cave Theatre (Horse Cave); Actors Theatre (Louisville); Shakespeare in Central Park (Louisville); Jenny Wiley Theatre (Prestonburg).

*Located in the foothills of the Appalachian Mountains, Berea is a well-known crafts center. Here local artisans demonstrate basket-weaving.*

# The Land and the Climate

Rich Kentucky bluegrass is considered ideal for commercial turf and pasture; it does not grow in any other state. Though it appears green most of the year, it puts forth blue blossoms in May. This unique vegetation earned Kentucky its nickname, the Bluegrass State.

Kentucky, the "Bluegrass State," gets its name from the luxuriant grass in the north-central area that bears blue-gray blossoms in the spring. Thoroughbred racehorses and rich tobacco have also made Kentucky famous.

The state has five main land regions. They are, from east to west, the Appalachian Plateau, the Bluegrass Region, the Pennyroyal Region, the Western Coal Field, and the East Gulf Coastal Plain.

The Appalachian Plateau on the eastern end of the state is part of a land formation that extends from New York State to Alabama; in Kentucky it is referred to as the Cumberland Plateau. Here are mountain ridges with high flatlands among them, valleys, rivers, and streams. In the southeastern section are peaks of the Appalachians, as well as of the Cumberland and Pine Mountain chains. Between the latter two chains is the Middlesboro Basin, with several valleys. The highest point in the state is in this region—Black Mountain, near Lynch, is 4,145 feet above sea level. Natural gas, oil, and choice timber are found here, and there are some corn and fruit farms.

The Bluegrass Region is in the north-central part of the state, west of the Appalachian Plateau, and extends into Ohio. The Ohio River borders this section on the north and west, and in the central Bluegrass are extensive pasturelands, where horses, cattle, and sheep are raised. Corn and tobacco farms are also in this area. The Bluegrass Region has the largest cities in the state, as well as most of its horse farms and manufacturing establishments. In the southern part of the Bluegrass are domelike knobs, which look like volcanic cones, and flood plains. This area is called the Knobs Region, and most of it is wooded.

The Pennyroyal Region is also called the Southwestern Mississippian Embayment, and it extends along the state's southern border

Cumberland Falls, in Corbin, descends through the mountainous region of the southern Appalachian Plateau.

Tobacco is the state's most important and profitable crop. Kentucky is the second-largest tobacco producer in the nation, second only to North Carolina.

from the Appalachian Plateau to Kentucky Lake. The region is named for a species of mint that is common in the area. In the southern Pennyroyal are vast farmlands where livestock, corn, hay, and tobacco are raised. There is a treeless area in the center of the region, known as The Barrens, where the Indians periodically burned the forests to provide grazing lands for the buffalo they hunted. The northern Pennyroyal has rocky ridges and bluffs, with thousands of miles of caves in the limestone rock of the area. The best known is Mammoth Cave, the center of a national park.

The Western Coal Field, in northwestern Kentucky, contains fertile valleys as well as high, rocky cliffs and wooded ridges. In addition to good farmland where hogs, fruit, tobacco, and hay are raised, the region contains about half of Kentucky's large coal reserves.

The East Gulf Coastal Plain is part of the strip of land that stretches from Florida west to Mississippi and north to Illinois. Kentuckians often call this western section of the state the Jackson Purchase Region, because military hero Andrew Jackson bought it from the Indians in 1818. Here there are wide flood plains covered by cypress swamps and many low hills. Cattle and soybean farms are common, and some pecans and cotton are grown here.

The Ohio River is the most important waterway in Kentucky; it flows along the entire northern border of the state. On the west is the Mississippi River. Other important rivers are the Big Sandy, the Tug Fork, the Cumberland, the Green, the Kentucky, the Licking, the Salt, and the Tennessee. The highest waterfall in the state is Cumberland Falls, on the Cumberland River, at 68 feet. The state has many lakes, the biggest of which are man-made. Dale Hollow Reservoir, on the Tennessee-Kentucky border, covers 30,000 acres. Kentucky Lake, in the western part of the state, is 185 miles long. Other man-made lakes include Barkley, Dewey, and Herrington Lakes.

Kentucky's climate is generally warm and rainy. In January temperatures rarely drop below 38 degrees Fahrenheit, and in July they rarely rise above 77 degrees F. Rain is heaviest in southern Kentucky, where total precipitation averages about 48 inches a year.

Mammoth Cave is perhaps the best-known natural feature of the northern Pennyroyal region, which has thousands of miles of limestone caves, ridges, and bluffs. The five levels of Mammoth Cave contain more than 150 miles of explored passageways.

The riverboat *Belle of Louisville* makes a nighttime journey down the Ohio River, Kentucky's most important waterway.

Kentucky's Bluegrass Region, in the north-central part of the state, is an ideal area for cultivating corn and tobacco but is best known for its legendary horse farms. Since the early 1800s, people have taken advantage of the prime pasturelands to produce many thoroughbred racing winners.

Daniel Boone's wilderness skills and bravery as an Indian fighter helped open the frontier for settlement. After years of hunting and exploring in the wilds of Kentucky, Boone led settlers through the Cumberland Gap in the Appalachian Mountains into central Kentucky and blazed the Wilderness Trail for the Transylvania Company. He defended Boonesboro and other nearby settlements against Indian attack during the Revolutionary War.

# The History

Indians were probably living in what was to become Kentucky as long as 15,000 years ago—most of them in the western forests. By the time the first white men arrived, the Cherokee, Delaware, Iroquois, and Shawnee tribes were among the largest in the region. There is a possibility that English and French explorers were the first Europeans to visit what is now Kentucky in the late 1600s and early 1700s. These included the Englishmen Colonel Abram Wood, Gabriel Arthur, and

John Peter Salley; and the Frenchmen Father Jacques Marquette, Louis Joliet, and Robert Cavelier. But the Kentucky territory was not settled until Thomas Walker, of what was then Fincastle County, Virginia, came through the Cumberland Gap in the Alleghenies in 1750 and built a home near what is now Barbourville.

Then, in 1767, came the great frontiersman Daniel Boone, and his "axe men." They blazed (marked a trail for) the Wilderness Road and set up headquarters in Boonesborough in 1775, after being driven out by the Indians in several early attempts. Boonesborough was not the first permanent settlement in the state, however. James Harrod established Kentucky's first town, Harrodsburg, in 1774, and a year later there were enough people to open the first legislature west of the Alleghenies. Kentucky County separated from Fincastle County, Virginia, in 1776, shortly after the American Revolution began.

The state's first courthouse, at Constitution Square in Danville, was the site at which the legislature planned Kentucky's declaration of independence from Virginia in 1784.

During the Revolutionary War, Indians who sided with the British attacked the Kentucky settlers repeatedly, but with the aid of Daniel Boone and frontier soldier George Rogers Clark, they were repelled. In 1778 Clark led attacks on three British posts and cut off British supplies to the Indians. That same year Clark founded a village on the Ohio River, which was named Louisville in honor of Louis XVI of France, who had helped the colonists during the Revolution. In 1779 a hunting party from Harrodsburg built a fort and blockhouse at a place they called Lexington, after the Revolutionary battlefield in Massachusetts.

Kentucky petitioned for statehood in 1790, and was admitted as the 15th state in 1792. The citizens of the state had founded the first college west of the Alleghenies, Transylvania, at Lexington, in 1780. Later they added the area's first medical school, law school, teacher training school, and library. The *Kentucky Gazette,* the first newspaper on its side of the mountains, began publication in 1787. The West's first railroad, the Lexington and Ohio, was built in 1830–32.

In the early 19th century, horse breeding and tobacco farming became important to the state's economy, and hemp, the plant used for making rope, was another income-producing crop. Because of the availability of corn, rye, and other grains, Kentucky became the center of whiskey production in the United States.

Maker's Mark distillery, in Loretto, is one of the oldest in the state and the only distillery to be named an official National Historic Landmark. Sour-mash whiskey has been made there since 1840, in the tradition that made Kentucky the national center of whiskey production more than a hundred years ago.

The explorer General George Rogers Clark fought in the Revolutionary War against the Indians who had sided with the British. A compatriot of Daniel Boone, Clark used the city of Louisville as a springboard for successful attacks on Forts Massac and Kaskaskia in 1778.

This mansion, called Whitehaven, was built in Paducah in 1866, in a grand style typical of the Civil War era. Paducah was the first Kentucky city to be occupied by Union troops, under General Ulysses S. Grant, in 1861.

The Civil War began in 1861, and Kentucky tried to stay neutral, since it had social, economic, and political ties with both the North and the South. It was a border state between the warring regions and was the birthplace of the presidents of both sides—Abraham Lincoln had been born near Hodgenville and Jefferson Davis near Fairview. Although a special convention claiming to represent 65 counties voted for secession, the regular legislature never did so. Nevertheless, fierce battles were fought on Kentucky soil, especially in the eastern part of the state, the most severe being the Confederate defeat at Perryville in 1862.

Confederate troops had invaded western Kentucky in the summer of 1861, and Union troops under the command of General Ulysses S. Grant occupied Paducah. In September of that year, the state legislature created a military force to drive out the Confederates in order to maintain the state's neutrality. As it turned out, some 75,000 Kentuckians fought in the Union Army, and about 35,000 fought in the Confederate Army.

After the war, however, Kentucky became more sympathetic to the

South than to the North. The state was affected by the depression that blanketed the South, since southern markets could no longer afford to buy Kentucky's products and the river ports were hard hit by the decline in traffic along the Ohio and Mississippi Rivers.

The outlook for Kentucky grew brighter toward the end of the 19th century. Burley tobacco was being cultivated in central and eastern Kentucky, and railroad construction had expanded so that the products of eastern Kentucky could be transported more efficiently. Timber harvesting and coal mining began to be more profitable. Many new horse farms were begun in the Bluegrass Region, where superior grazing had already attracted numerous livestock producers.

The Great Depression of the 1930s hit Kentucky even harder than most other states. Many coal miners were unemployed when mines closed down, and small farms were given up by families who sought work in the cities. Federal conservation projects and state road construction provided some employment.

The industrial demand created by World War II made Kentucky mines and farms productive once more, and the state began to shift from an agricultural to a manufacturing center. The industrial growth that began in the 1940s continues today, but the eastern part of the state still has economic troubles, mainly because the demand for coal continues to decline. Even so, more than 65 percent of the value of goods produced in Kentucky comes from manufacturing or processing. The state leads the nation in the production of whiskey, with principal distilleries located in Louisville, Lexington, Bardstown, and Owensboro. Other important manufacturing areas are chemical and allied products, electrical machinery, tobacco products, and meats. In 1966 a civil rights act was passed by the Kentucky Legislature. It prohibited discriminatory hiring practices by companies with more than eight employees and made discrimination in public accommodations illegal. Kentucky was the first southern state to pass such a law.

# Education

The first schools in Kentucky were founded by churches. The Transylvania Seminary opened in Danville in 1785 and eventually became Transylvania University—one of the first universities in the United States. The University of Louisville, founded in 1837, is the oldest city university in the United States. Due to poverty and a lack of economic support, many of Kentucky's educational institutions are not equivalent to those elsewhere in the United States. Louisville, Kentucky, was the first large southern city to admit blacks to previously all-white schools, though the process has often been slow. Sixty-six school districts filed a lawsuit against the state of Kentucky because the funding of public schools is based on local property taxes, which is discriminatory. In 1990, the Kentucky Supreme Court ordered the General Assembly to design a new public school system to distribute the funds fairly. There are twenty-eight colleges and universities in Kentucky.

# The People

Slightly more than half the people in the state of Kentucky now live in urban areas, most of them in the metropolitan areas of Ashland, Lexington, and Louisville. A significant number of Kentuckians live in the metropolitan areas of nearby Cincinnati, Ohio, and Evansville, Indiana. Almost all the residents of the state were born in the United States, and the largest single religious body in the state is Southern Baptist, although there are many members of the Disciples of Christ, the Methodist, the Presbyterian, and the Roman Catholic churches.

*Below:*
Jefferson Davis, born in Todd County, was the only president of the Confederate States of America. After he was chosen provisional president of the Confederacy in February 1861, Davis led the fight for the preservation of slavery and the right of southern states to secede from the Union. His reluctance to accept advice, and his stubborn loyalty toward friends who proved incompetent in warfare, were his major downfalls. Davis did recognize the military genius of General Robert E. Lee, whom he made commander-in-chief of the Confederate armies, but the southern cause lacked the resources to pursue the Civil War to a victorious conclusion.

*Above:*
Abraham Lincoln, 16th president of the United States, was born in a log cabin near present-day Hodgenville. On January 1, 1863, two years after the start of the Civil War, President Lincoln issued the Emancipation Proclamation, which freed the slaves. Later that year, on the site of the great battle at Gettysburg, Pennsylvania, the president delivered his Gettysburg Address, recalling from the Declaration of Independence that the United States was dedicated to the proposition that "all men are created equal" and stating that the outcome of the war would determine the fate of democracy. Lincoln lived to see his Union's victory in the war, but was unable to preside over the painful period of Reconstruction, during which he had hoped to help the southern states recover from the conflict. The president's life came to a tragic end on April 14, 1865, when he was shot and killed by John Wilkes Booth in a Washington, D.C. theater.

## Famous People

Many famous people were born in the state of Kentucky. Here are a few:

**Muhammad Ali** b.1942, Louisville. Heavyweight boxing champion

**Alben W. Barkley** 1877-1956, Graves County. Vice-president under Harry Truman

**Judge Roy Bean** 1825-1903, Mason County. Frontier judge

**Louis Brandeis** 1856-1941, Louisville. Supreme Court justice

**John C. Breckenridge** 1821-1875, near Lexington. Vice-president under James Buchanan and Confederate general

**Sophonisba Breckenridge** 1866-1948, Lexington. Woman suffrage activist

**John Y. Brown** b.1933, Lexington. Owner of Kentucky Fried Chicken and governor

**Simon Bolivar Buckner** 1823-1914, near Munfordville.

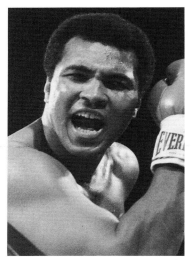

*Born Cassius Clay, Muhammad Ali began boxing at age 12. His first match, which he won, was televised on the program "Champions of Tomorrow."*

Confederate general

**Simon Bolivar Buckner, Jr.** 1886-1945, Munfordville. World War II general

**John Buford** 1826-1863, Woodford County. Union general

**Jim Bunning** b. 1931, Southgate. Baseball player and representative from Kentucky

**Kit Carson** 1809-1868, Madison County. Frontiersman and scout

**Steve Cauthen** b.1960, Covington. Jockey

**Edgar Cayce** 1877-1945, Hopkinsville. Healer and seer

**William Conrad** b.1920, Louisville. Television actor: *Cannon, Jake and the Fat Man*

**Dave Cowens** b.1948, Newport. Basketball player

**Jefferson Davis** 1808-1889, Fairview. President of the Confederate States of America

**Thomas C. Du Pont** 1863-1930, Louisville. Consolidated E. I. Du Pont de Nemours

**Irene Dunne** 1898-1990 Louisville. Film actress: *Anna and the King of Siam, I Remember Mama*

**Don Everly** b.1937, Brownie. Rock-and-roll singer

**Phil Everly** b.1938, Brownie. Rock-and-roll singer

**Red Foley** 1910-1968, Blue Lick. Country-and-western singer

**Crystal Gayle** b. 1951, Paintsville. Country-and-western singer

**D. W. Griffith** 1875-1948, near Beard's Station. Silent-film producer and director: *The Birth of a Nation, Intolerance*

**John Marshall Harlan** 1833-1911, Boyle County. Supreme Court justice

*The Everly Brothers had two big hits in 1957, "Wake Up, Little Susie" and "Bye-Bye Love."*

**Duncan Hines** 1880-1959, Bowling Green. Gourmet

**John Bell Hood** 1831-1879, Owingsville. Confederate general

**Paul Hornung** b.1935, Louisville. Hall of Fame football player

**Husband E. Kimmel** 1882-1968, Henderson. Admiral in charge of the Pearl Harbor Naval Base at the time of the Japanese attack

**Arthur Krock** 1886-1974, Glasgow. Four-time Pulitzer Prize-winning newspaper correspondent

**Abraham Lincoln** 1809-1865, Larue County. Sixteenth President of the United States

**Loretta Lynn** b.1932, Butcher Hollow. Country-and-western singer

**Victor Mature** b.1916, Louisville. Film actor: *Samson and Delilah, Firepower*

**Thomas Hunt Morgan** 1866-1945, Lexington. Nobel Prize-winning geneticist

**Carry Nation** 1846-1911, Garrard County. Temperance worker who organized a branch of the WCTU.

**Patricia Neal** b.1926, Packard. Academy Award-winning actress: *Hud, The Hasty Heart*

**John Patrick** b.1905, Louisville. Pulitzer Prize-winning playwright: *Teahouse of the August Moon, Everybody Loves Opal*

**John Pope** 1822-1892, Louisville. Union general

**Diane Sawyer** b.1945, Glasgow. Television newswoman

**Jesse Stuart** 1907-1984, near Riverton. Poet and novelist: *The Threat That Runs True, Taps for Private Tussie*

**Allen Tate** 1899-1979, Winchester. Critic and poet: *The Fathers*

**Helen Thomas** b.1920, Winchester. First woman chief of the UPI White House bureau

**Wes Unseld** b.1946,
Louisville. Hall of Fame
basketball player
**Fred Vinson** 1890-1953,
Louisa. Supreme Court
chief justice
**Robert Penn Warren** 1905-

*Diane Sawyer was a member of
Richard Nixon's press staff during
his administration. After his
resignation from the presidency, she
helped him compile his memoirs.*

1989, Guthrie. Three-time
Pulitzer Prize-winning
novelist and poet: *All the
King's Men, Promises*
**Whitney Young** 1921-1971,
Lincoln Ridge. Civil rights
leader

**Colleges and Universities**
There are many colleges and
universities in Kentucky.
Here are the more prominent,
with their locations, dates of
founding, and enrollments.
*Asbury College,* Wilmore, 1890,
1,129
*Bellarmine College,* Louisville,
1950, 2,326
*Berea College,* Berea, 1855,
1,563
*Centre College,* Danville, 1819,
860
*Eastern Kentucky University,*
Richmond, 1906, 16,866
*Georgetown College,*
Georgetown, 1829, 1,476
*Kentucky State University,*

Frankfort, 1886, 2,545
*Morehead State University,*
Morehead, 1922, 9,169
*Murray State University,*
Murray, 1922, 8,190
*Spalding University,* Louisville,
1829, 1,141
*Transylvania University,*
Lexington, 1780, 963
*Union College,* Barbourville,
1879, 1,147
*University of Kentucky,*
Lexington, 1865, 24,197
*University of Louisville,* 1798,
10,228
*Western Kentucky University,*
Bowling Green, 1906,
15,750

**Where To Get More
Information**
The Department of Travel
Development
2200 Capital Plaza Tower
Frankfort, KY 40601
Or call 1-800-225-8747

# Tennessee

There is no official state seal of Tennessee; the legislature has never adopted one. The unofficial seal is similar to one recommended in 1801 by a special committee. It is circular, and on it are a plow, a sheaf of wheat, and a cotton plant (to symbolize agriculture), and a river boat (to symbolize commerce). Above the wheat is the Roman numeral XVI (Tennessee was the 16th state). Under the wheat, plow, and cotton plant appears the word "Agriculture"; under the boat is the word "Commerce." Surrounding the pictures is a circle that bears the inscription, "The Great Seal of the State of Tennessee," and "1796," the date of the first state constitution.

# TENNESSEE

## At a Glance

**State Flag**

**Capital:** Nashville

**State Bird:** Mockingbird

**Major Industries:** Manufacturing of chemicals, textiles, machinery, construction, transportation, livestock

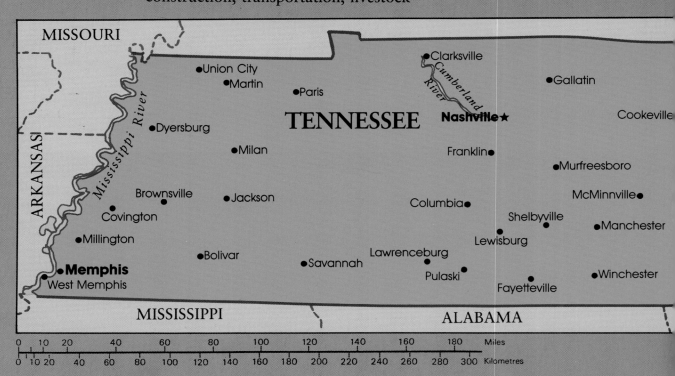

**Size:** 42,144 square miles (34th largest)
**Population:** 5,023,990 (17th largest)

**Major Crops:** Soybeans, tobacco, wheat, corn, cotton
**State Motto:** Agriculture and Commerce

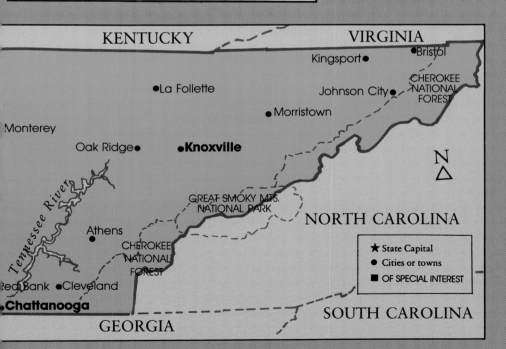

KENTUCKY    VIRGINIA

●Bristol

Kingsport●

●La Follette

Johnson City● CHEROKEE
NATIONAL
FOREST

●Morristown

Monterey

Oak Ridge● ●**Knoxville**

N
△

GREAT SMOKY MTS.
NATIONAL PARK

NORTH CAROLINA

Athens
●

CHEROKEE
NATIONAL
FOREST

★ State Capital
● Cities or towns
■ OF SPECIAL INTEREST

Red Bank ●Cleveland

**Chattanooga**

GEORGIA    SOUTH CAROLINA

Tennessee River

**State Flower:** Iris

**State Tree:** Tulip Poplar
**Nickname:** Volunteer State
**State Song:**
"The Tennessee Waltz"

### State Flag

The state flag has a red background. In the center is a blue circle bearing three white stars (standing for East, Middle, and Western Tennessee) surrounded by a white circle. At the far end of the flag are two small stripes running from top to bottom—one white and one blue. The flag was designed by LeRoy Reeves and adopted in 1905.

### State Motto

*Agriculture and Commerce*

Tennessee has no official motto, since the state legislature has never adopted one. But these words appear on the state seal.

### State Slogan

*Tennessee—America at Its Best*

In 1965, the legislature adopted this slogan.

*This view of the Great Smoky Mountains shows clearly the blue haze that gives the mountain range its name.*

## State Name and Nicknames

The name for Tennessee came from the Cherokee Indian word "Tanasi," whose meaning is unknown. (The Indians had called two villages and the river they bordered—now the Little Tennessee River—Tanasi.)

The most common nickname for Tennessee is the *Volunteer State*, because of the brave volunteers from Tennessee who fought with Andrew Jackson in the Battle of New Orleans at the end of the War of 1812. It is also called the *Big Bend State* for the bend in the Tennessee River, and the *Mother of Southwestern Statesmen* for the three Presidents who were born there. Two other nicknames, the *Hog State* and the *Hominy State*, are seldom used today.

## State Capital

The first capital of Tennessee was Knoxville (1792 to 1806). For one day in 1807 it was Kingston, and then Knoxville again (1807-12). The capital then alternated between Murfreesboro and Nashville until, in 1843, Nashville was made the permanent capital.

## State Cultivated Flower

In 1919, it was decided that Tennessee's schoolchildren should pick the state flower, and the passion flower, *Passiflora incarnata*, was chosen. But in 1933, the state legislature named the iris (family *Iridaceae*) the state flower without repealing the previous choice. It wasn't until 1973 that the iris was designated the only official state cultivated flower.

## State Wildflower

Tennessee was still left with a question of what to do about the passion flower. So the same 1973 resolution that made the iris the state cultivated flower named the passion flower as the state wildflower. The name "passion flower" came from early Christian missionaries to South America, who saw such sacred symbols as the crown of thorns and three crosses within the flower. It is also called the maypop, the wild apricot, and the ocoee (the Indian name for the plant).

## State Tree

In 1947, the tulip poplar, *Liriodendron tulipifera*, was adopted as the state tree. Other names for the tree are the tulip tree, yellow poplar, the hickory poplar, the basswood, the cucumber tree, the tulipwood, the whitewood, the white poplar, the poplar, and the old-wife's-shirt tree.

## State Bird

In 1933, the people of Tennessee voted for their favorite bird. Among the choices were the mockingbird, robin, cardinal, bobwhite, and bluebird. The mockingbird, *Mimus polyglottos*, was named the official state bird.

## State Fine Art

Porcelain painting, selected

in 1981, is the state fine art.

**State Folk Dance**
In 1980, the square dance was named as state folk dance.

**State Gem**
The Tennessee pearl was adopted as state gem in 1979.

**State Insects**
Tennessee has two state insects, both selected in 1975—the firefly (*Photinus scintillans*) and the ladybug or ladybird (*Hippodamia convergens*).

**State Language**
English was named the state language in 1984.

**State Poem**
In 1973, "Oh Tennessee, My Tennessee," by Admiral William Lawrence, was adopted as the state poem.

**State Railroad Museum**
The Tennessee Valley Railroad Museum was named the state railroad

*One of Tennessee's state insects, the ladybug.*

museum in 1978.

**State Rock**
The state rock, limestone, was selected in 1979.

**State Wild Animal**
The raccoon, *Procyon lotor*, was named state wild animal in 1972.

**State Songs**
Tennessee has five state songs. They are: "My Homeland, Tennessee," by Nell Grayson Taylor and Roy Lamont (adopted in 1925); "When It's Iris Time in

Tennessee," by Willa Mae Ward (1935); "My Tennessee," by Francis Hannah Tranum (1955); "The Tennessee Waltz," by Redd Stewart and Pee Wee King (1965); and "Rocky Top," by Boudleaux and Felice Bryant (1982).

**Population**
The population of Tennessee in 1992 was 5,023,990, making it the 17th most populous state. There are 121.9 persons per square mile. Just over 25 percent of Tennessee's population is employed in the manufacturing sector. This is the third highest percentage of all the United States.

**Industries**
The principal industries of the state of Tennessee are trade, services, construction, transportation, communication, public utilities, finance, insurance, and real estate. The chief products are chemicals, food products, nonelectrical

machinery, electric and electronic equipment, apparel, fabricated metal products, rubber products, plastics, and paper products.

**Agriculture**

The chief crops of the state are soybeans, tobacco, wheat, cotton, and corn. Tennessee is also a livestock state, and there are estimated to be

some 2.3 million cattle, 770,000 hogs and pigs, and 1.72 million chickens and turkeys on its farms. Red oak, yellow poplar, white oak, and hickory are harvested for lumber; and crushed stone and zinc are important mineral resources.

**Government**

The governor of Tennessee

serves a four-year term. The speaker of the senate also holds the job of lieutenant governor, and most of the other administrative officers are appointed either by the governor, the state legislature, or the state supreme court. The attorney general is elected. The state legislature, which meets in odd-numbered years, consists of a 33-member senate and a 99-member house of representatives, all of them elected by districts. The most recent state constitution was adopted in 1870. In addition to its two U.S. senators, Tennessee has nine representatives in the U.S. House of Representatives. The state has 11 votes in the electoral college.

**Sports**

Many sporting events on the collegiate and secondary school levels are played all over the state. On the collegiate level, the University of Tennessee won

*Federal Express, one of the largest service industries in the country, offers midnight tours of this Superhub facility in Memphis.*

the Sugar Bowl in 1943, 1971, 1986, and 1991, the Cotton Bowl in 1951 and 1990, and the Orange Bowl in 1939. The women's basketball team at the same university won the NCAA national championship in 1987 and in 1989.

## Major Cities

*Chattanooga* (population 152,494). Settled in 1835, Chattanooga was originally a Cherokee Indian outpost. The Indians called it "Tsatanugi," or rock coming to a point. This was a description of Lookout Mountain, which overlooks the city. The creek that runs here the Indians called "Chickamauga," or river of blood, which became an apt description during the Civil War when the two sides, in the Battle of Chickamauga, suffered more than 34,000 casualties. Today, Chattanooga is a thriving, wealthy city with more than 600 major industries.

*Places to visit in Chattanooga:* Hunter Museum of Art,

*Chucalissa Indian Village, reconstructed after archaeological digs in the 1950s and 1960s, is representative of Indian life along the shores of the Mississippi.*

Houston Museum, Tennessee Valley Railroad Museum, National Knife Museum, Chattanooga Choo-Choo, Lookout Mountain Incline Railway, Lookout Mountain, Point Park, Cravens House (1856), Ruby Falls-Lookout Mountain Caverns, Rock City Gardens, Reflection Riding and Chattanooga Nature Center, Confederama, Signal Mountain, Raccoon Mountain Caverns, and Raccoon Mountain Pumped Storage Facility.

*Knoxville* (population 165,039). Settled in 1786, Knoxville was the first capital of Tennessee. A frontier outpost on the edge of the Cherokee Indian nation, it was founded by a Revolutionary War veteran from North Carolina, who named it after Secretary of War Henry Knox. During the Civil War the city was seized by the Confederates. Then, in 1863, the Union Army occupied it, and the Confederates began a siege. The Union army won the battle, but large sections of the city were destroyed. Today, Knoxville is an education center and the major manufacturing city in the East Tennessee Valley.

*Places to visit in Knoxville:* Governor William Blount Mansion (1792), Craighead-Jackson House (1818), Ramsey House (1795), Confederate Memorial Hall, Knoxville Museum of Art, East Tennessee Historical Center, General James White's Fort (1786), Beck Cultural Exchange Center, Students' Museum, John Sevier Historic Site, Crescent Bend (1834), Knoxville Zoological Park, Frank H. McClung Museum, and University Arboretum.

*Memphis* (population 610,337). Settled in 1819, it was named by General James Winchester after the Egyptian city of Memphis, which means "place of good abode." It was laid out by Andrew Jackson and John Overton on a land grant from North Carolina. River traffic quickly

*The Incline Railway, built in 1895, connects Chattanooga with the summit of Lookout Mountain. The mile-long cable-car system has a steep grade of 72.7 degrees.*

developed, and, for a short time, Memphis was the Confederate capital of Tennessee. After the Civil War, the city was plagued by yellow fever epidemics. One of them nearly wiped out the community in 1878, killing more than two-thirds of its residents. Memphis became a village after this disaster, and did not take on a city charter again until 1893. By 1892 Memphis had become the

busiest inland cotton market and the hardwood lumber center of the world. Today it is a towering metropolis with some 800 industrial plants.

*Places to visit in Memphis:* Mud Island, Memphis Brooks Museum of Art, Memphis Zoo and Aquarium, Memphis Pink Palace Museum and Planetarium, Dixon Gallery and Gardens, Victorian Village, Magevney House (1837), Woodruff-Fontaine House (1870), Mallory-Neely

House (1855), music clubs, Beale Street Historic District, Graceland, National Ornamental Metal Museum, Lichterman Nature Center, Libertyland, Memphis Belle, T.O. Fuller State Park, Chucalissa Indian Village and Museum, and Meeman-Shelby Forest State Park.

*Nashville* (population 488,374). Settled in 1779, the capital city was established by a band of pioneers who built a fort on the west bank of the Cumberland River—Fort Nashborough. The city was taken by Union forces in 1862 during the Civil War. Today it is a booming business city and the largest banking center in the South. It also has some 700 industries. Because of its many colleges and universities, its many churches, and its book publishing activities, it is often called the "Athens of the South."

*Places to visit in Nashville:* State Capitol (1845-1859), Tennessee State Museum, Military Museum, Fort Nashborough, Cumberland Museum and Science Center, the Country Music Wax Museum and Shopping Mall, The Parthenon, Upper Room, Hermitage (1819), Tulip Grove (1836), Belle Meade (1853), Belmont Mansion, Travellers' Rest Historic House (1799), Tennessee Botanical Gardens and Fine Arts Center, Museum of Tobacco Art and History, Country Music Hall of Fame and Museum, RCA Studio B, Opryland, The Grand Ole Opry, Grand Ole Opry Tours, Ryman Auditorium and Museum, Minnie Pearl's Museum, Barbara Mandrell Country, Music Valley Wax Museum of Stars, Jim Reeves Museum, Waylon's Private Collection, George Jones' Car Collectors Hall of Fame, Oscar Farris Agricultural Museum, and Radnor Lake State Natural Area.

**Places to Visit**
  The National Park Service maintains nine areas in the State of Tennessee: Stones River National Battlefield,

*The gates to Graceland, Elvis Presley's home, feature the opening notes of "Love Me Tender," one of his early hits.*

Fort Donelson National Battlefield, Great Smoky Mountains National Park, Andrew Johnson National Historic Site, Natchez Trace Parkway, Cumberland Gap National Historical Park, Shiloh National Military Park and Cemetary, and Cherokee National Forest. In addition, there are 35 state recreation areas.

*Columbia*: President James K. Polk Ancestral Home. Built in 1816, this Federal-style house contains furniture and portraits once used in the White House.

*Dayton*: Rhea County Courthouse. The famous Scopes trial was held in this building, built in 1891.

*Elizabethton*: Sycamore Shoals State Historic Area. A replica of Fort Watauga, with five buildings and palisade walls, was reconstructed here.

*Franklin*: Carnton Mansion. One of the most elegant estates in the area, it was built in 1826 and served as a hospital during the Civil War battle at Franklin.

*Greenville*: Davy Crockett Birthplace Park. A reproduction of the log cabin in which Crockett was born.

*Harrogate*: Abraham Lincoln Museum. This contains one of the largest groupings of Lincoln and Civil War materials in the world.

*Jackson*: "Casey" Jones Home and Railroad Museum. The original house of the famous engineer and railroad memorabilia are displayed.

*Johnson City*: Tipton-Haynes Historical Farm. A restored farm.

*Kingsport*: Exchange Place. A restored nineteenth-century farm and crafts center.

*Maryville*: Sam Houston Schoolhouse. The restored schoolhouse where Sam Houston taught in 1812.

*Morristown*: Crockett Tavern and Museum. A reproduction of the tavern that Davy Crockett's father operated in the 1790s—Crockett's boyhood home.

*Murfreesboro*: Cannonsburgh Pioneer Village. A reconstructed village.

*Norris*: Norris Dam and Lake. The 265-foot high and 1,860-foot long dam was the first one built by the TVA.

*Oak Ridge*: American Museum

*The Hermitage, the home of Andrew Jackson, was built between 1819 and 1831 of bricks fired on the property.*

*Sam Davis's boyhood home, just outside Smyrna. During the Civil War, Davis was captured by Union troops while carrying secret information about fortifications and Confederate troop movements. Refusing to reveal any information to his captors, he was hanged as a spy at the age of 21. For this, he is remembered as the "boy hero of the Confederacy."*

of Science and Energy. One of the world's largest energy exhibitions, the museum displays exhibits on fossil fuels and energy alternatives.

*Sweetwater*: Lost Sea. The world's largest underground lake can be explored in glass-bottomed boats.

*Townsend*: Tuckaleechee Caverns. The caves contain a cathedral-like main chamber and the largest cavern room in the eastern United States.

*Vonore*: Fort Loudoun. This restored fort represents the southwestern outpost of England during the French and Indian War.

*Winchester*: Hundred Oaks Castle. Built in 1890, this 30-room structure features a library that is a replica of the one in Sir Walter Scott's castle in Abbotsford, Scotland.

### Events

There are many events and organizations that schedule activities of various kinds in the state of Tennessee. Here are some of them.

*Sports*: Grand Prix of Chattanooga (Chattanooga), Walking Horse Show (Clarksville); Knoxville Watersports Festival (Knoxville);

*This log cabin was the birthplace of Davy Crockett, the legendary frontiersman and soldier.*

*The Grand Ole Opry House is now home to the weekly country and western radio broadcasts that began in 1925.*

International Grand Championship Walking Horse Show (Murfreesboro); Iroquois Steeplechase (Nashville); Longhorn Rodeo (Nashville); Nashville Motor Raceway (Nashville); Tennessee Walking Horse National Celebration (Shelbyville).

*Arts and Crafts*: Rhododendron Festival (Elizabethton); Spring Wild Flower Pilgrimage (Gatlinburg); East Tennessee Antique Dealers' Show (Kingsport); Dogwood Arts Festival (Knoxville); Artfest (Knoxville); Murfreesboro Antiques Show and Sale (Murfreesboro); Tuckaleechee Cove Arts, Crafts and Music Festival (Townsend).

*Music*: Chattanooga Symphony (Chattanooga); Riverbend Festival (Chattanooga); Chattanooga Opera Association (Chattanooga); Mid-South Jazz Festival (Clarksville); Blue Grass Festival (Elizabethton); Old-Time Country Radio Reunion (Jonesborough); Knoxville Symphony (Knoxville); Opera Memphis (Memphis); Memphis Symphony (Memphis); Beale Street Music Festival (Memphis); Memphis Music Festival (Memphis); National Blues Music Awards (Memphis); Nashville Symphony (Nashville); Summer Lights Festival (Nashville); International Country Music Fan Fair (Nashville); Grand Master Old-Time Fiddling Championship (Nashville); National Quartet Convention (Nashville); Appalachian Music and Craft Festival (Oak Ridge); Sewanee Summer Music Center Concerts (Sewanee).

*Entertainment*: Autumn Leaf Special (Chattanooga); Fall Color Cruise (Chattanooga); Madrigal Feasts (Clarksville); Mule Day (Columbia); National Tennessee Walking Horse Jubilee (Columbia); Maury Country Fair (Columbia); Cumberland County Fair (Crossville); Old-Timers' Day (Dickson); Covered Bridge Celebration (Elizabethton); Overmountain Victory Trail Celebration (Elizabethton); Scottish Festival and Games (Gatlinburg); Folk Festival of the Smokies (Gatlinburg); Christmas Festival (Gatlinburg); Historic Jonesborough Days (Jonesborough); Appalachian Fair (Johnson City); National Storytelling Festival (Jonesborough); Tennessee Valley Fair (Knoxville); Memphis in May International Festival (Memphis); Great River Carnival (Memphis); Elvis Presley International Tribute Week (Memphis); Mid-South Fair and Exposition (Memphis); Street Festival and Folkfest (Murfreesboro); Tennessee State Fair (Nashville); World's Biggest Fish Fry (Paris).

*Tours*: Maury County Spring Tour (Columbia); Carter County Wild Flower Tour (Elizabethton); Heritage Foundation Town and Country Tour (Franklin); Carter House Christmas Candle Light Tour (Franklin); Sumner County Pilgrimage (Gallatin); Rugby Pilgrimage (Rugby); Christmas in Olde Jonesborough (Johnson City).

*Theater*: Tivoli Theater (Chattanooga); Little Theater (Chattanooga); Backstage Playhouse (Chattanooga); Cumberland County Playhouse (Crossville); Outdoor Drama (Elizabethton); Sweet Fanny Adams Theater (Gatlinburg); Carousel Theater (Knoxville); Clarence Brown Theater (Knoxville); Playhouse on the Square (Memphis); Circuit Playhouse (Memphis); Theatre Memphis (Memphis); "Smoky Mountain Passion Play" (Townsend); "Damascus Road" (Townsend).

*Much of Tennessee's music has its roots in the traditional folk songs of Appalachia. Bluegrass festivals and fiddling jamborees are among the state's favorite musical celebrations.*

## The Land and the Climate

The Great Smoky Mountains, in easternmost Tennessee, have numerous peaks that rise more than a mile above sea level. Clingmans Dome reaches an elevation of more than two miles and is the state's highest point. The Smoky Mountains are part of the Blue Ridge region.

Tennessee is handsomely rugged and rough-hewn. A mountainous land, it is a state of much variety—country ballads and big-city ballet, water-powered mills and atomic-energy plants.

The state has seven main land regions: the Blue Ridge, the Appalachian Ridge and Valley, the Appalachian Plateau, the Highland Rim, the Nashville Basin, the Gulf Coastal Plain, and the Mississippi Alluvial Plain.

The Blue Ridge is a narrow strip along the eastern border of the state; its average elevation is 5,000 feet above sea level. Tennessee's tallest mountain, Clingmans Dome at 6,642 feet high is located here. Some of the mountain ranges in the area are the Bald, Chilhowee, Great Smoky, Holston, Iron, Roan, Stone, and Unicoi Mountains. The Blue Ridge has a large amount of timber and some mineral resources.

The Appalachian Ridge and Valley forms another line from north to south west of the Blue Ridge. This 55-mile strip is a land of fertile farms in valleys between the ridges, many of them raising poultry, grapes, and fruit. The valleys and rivers in the eastern part of the region are called, collectively, the Great Valley.

The Appalachian Plateau, another north-south strip located west of the Appalachian Ridge and Valley, is also called the Cumberland Plateau. Here there are rocky cliffs ranging from 1,500 to 1,800 feet high. The region contains flat-topped mountains and deep, V-shaped valleys. Lookout Mountain, on the southern border, is located in this region. This is the land of the coal mines of Tennessee, and there are some fruit and potato farms.

The Highland Rim covers most of the central part of the state and runs north to south from border to border. In its eastern section are many caves, and in the central section are steep cliffs that slope into the Nashville Basin. Cattle, sheep, and vegetables are raised here.

*Above:*
Caney Falls is typical of the majestic cascades, deep gorges, and chasms found in the rocky Appalachian Plateau region. Nearby Fall Creek Falls is one of the highest waterfalls in America, at 256 feet.

*At left:*
The sun sets on the Mississippi River. The river defines the entire western border of Tennessee.

*Above:*
A large pumpkin harvest is collected on a Tennessee farm.

*At right:*
A proud farmer displays his fresh turnips.

*Far right:*
A young girl holds a bundle of sun-dried tobacco leaves. Historically, tobacco has been one of the state's most profitable crops, second only to cotton.

The Nashville Basin is an oval-shaped region located in the center of the Highland Rim. Here are rich farming areas where cattle and truck crops are raised. A large amount of phosphate is mined in the district.

The Gulf Coastal Plain is part of the same plain that runs from the Gulf of Mexico to southern Illinois. It extends from the Highland Rim westward almost to the Mississippi River and supports farms that raise corn, berries, poultry, soybeans, and peanuts. Dairy products, hogs, and poultry, as well as forest products are also produced here.

The Mississippi Alluvial Plain is a narrow strip that lies along the western border of the state. This low land, averaging less than 300 feet above sea level, is part of a larger strip that starts at the Gulf of Mexico. This area is also called the Mississippi Bottoms, and it is a fertile region where cotton, vegetables, and soybeans are grown.

Tennessee has three great river systems—the Mississippi, the Cumberland, and the Tennessee. Since 1933 the Tennessee Valley Authority and the United States Army Corps of Engineers have built many dams along the Cumberland and Tennessee Rivers and their tributaries, forming man-made lakes. The largest of these is Kentucky Lake; some of the others are Boone, Cherokee, Chickamauga, Douglas, Fort Loudoun, Fort Patrick Henry, Norris, Pickwick, Watauga, and Watts Bar Reservoirs. Taken together, these lakes are sometimes called the Great Lakes of the South.

Because it has a fairly warm, humid climate, Tennessee receives only four to six inches of snow yearly in the west, and about ten inches in the east. Temperatures range from 70 to 90 degrees Fahrenheit in July (higher in the western sections), and from 30 to 48 degrees F. in January.

The caves of the Highland Rim in central Tennessee are popular with exploring hikers and campers.

Much of Tennessee's country music extols traditional values, and working the land is a time-honored tradition in the state. Though manufacturing is now more important than agriculture, Tennessee initially grew prosperous from its rich soil, which made it a center of cotton production.

# The History

The prehistoric Indians called Mound Builders lived about 1,000 years ago in what was to become Tennessee. They built extensive earthen mounds to support their temples and chiefs' houses, and when the white man arrived in the middle of the 16th century, mounds were still being built by some members of the Cherokee and Chickasaw tribes who had settled in the area. Middle Tennessee was the hunting ground of the Cherokee, and one of their branches, the Chickamauga, lived near where Chattanooga now stands. In the west were the Chickasaw.

The earliest known date for the European exploration of Tennessee is 1541, when, it is believed, Hernando de Soto and a party of Spanish explorers planted the flag of Spain on the banks of the Mississippi River after their trek from Florida. This ceremony took place at the site of what is now Memphis.

After de Soto left, no white men visited the area until 1673. It was in that year that two Englishmen, James Needham and Gabriel Arthur, explored the Tennessee River Valley, and two Frenchmen, Louis Joliet of Canada and Father Jacques Marquette of France, descended the Mississippi River by boat.

Robert Cavelier (sometimes called Robert La Salle) came to the area in 1682 and claimed the entire Mississippi River Valley for France. He built Fort Prud'homme on the Chickasaw Bluffs, but it was so far from anything else in their New World holdings that the French abandoned it. However, the fertile Mississippi Valley soon began to attract more settlers from France. They called the area New France, and in 1714 Charles Charleville opened a trading post at French Lick, near present-day Nashville.

By the early 18th century not only France, but Spain and England claimed the region, and the three countries began to compete for the trade and friendship of the Indians. After Spain dropped out of the

Sequoya, a Cherokee Indian born in the Indian town of Taskigi, Tennessee, invented a system of writing for his people based on a set of 85 characters adapted to their spoken language. After 12 years of work, Sequoya's alphabet was accepted by Cherokee leaders (and later adapted to other Indian languages). For the first time, native Americans could publish books and newspapers in their own languages, and many learned to read.

competition, France and England resumed the French and Indian War that had been going on intermittently for years. The English won the war, and France turned over the land to them (1763), but meanwhile many lives had been lost in the years of conflict.

Tennessee native David "Davy" Crockett was a legendary hunter and woodsman who became a representative to the state legislature in 1821. Crockett had served as a scout for Andrew Jackson in the Creek War (1813–14) and led pioneers through the Tennessee wilderness as far west as the Mississippi River. An expert rifleman, he was said to have killed 105 bears within nine months. In 1827 he was elected to Congress, where he served three terms in the House of Representatives. In 1836 he went to Texas, where he was killed in the famous battle at the Alamo.

A replica of the six-room tavern and house built near Morristown by John Crockett, Davy's father, in the 1790s.

After 1763 the area really began opening up to settlement, with many pioneers coming in from Virginia and North Carolina. Although Tennessee was considered part of the North Carolina Colony, the eastern mountains made it difficult to govern. In 1775 a group called the Transylvania Company bought a large area of land from the Cherokees and hired Daniel Boone to blaze a trail through the Cumberland Gap. Frontiersman Davy Crockett, whose feats have been immortalized in stories, songs, and movies, was born on the new land a few years later.

Several Revolutionary War battles were fought in Tennessee, although the major conflict was between the whites and the Indians, who held out against the seizure of their land until the 1830s, when they had to give up the unequal struggle. In 1780 a group of settlers led by John Sevier crossed the Great Smoky Mountains into South Carolina to fight in the Battle of Kings Mountain, which the Americans won. In 1784 three counties in the eastern part of the territory broke off from North Carolina and formed the independent state of

A riverboat makes its way down the Cumberland River near Tennessee's capital city, Nashville, in 1849.

Franklin, making Sevier the governor. The state was never formally recognized; North Carolina took it back in 1788 and turned it over to the United States the following year. Tennessee thus became a new territory called the Territory of the United States South of the River Ohio. It became the 16th state in the Union in 1796, and its first governor was Sevier. At the time the population stood at about 77,000.

Two major factors in the early growth of the state were the cotton industry—for which much of the state's soil was ideally suited—and the Mississippi River, which could link that industry with distant markets. Memphis gradually became (and remains) one of the world's leading cotton markets.

During the War of 1812 with Great Britain, Tennessee riflemen volunteered in such great numbers that the state was nicknamed "the Volunteer State." Tennessean Andrew Jackson emerged from that war as a national hero for his defeat of the Creek Indians and his triumph over the British in the Battle of New Orleans.

As President, Jackson supported efforts to move the last of Tennessee's Indians out of the state. The treaty of New Echota forced thousands of Cherokees and other tribes to move west in 1838; so many died along the way that their route became known as the "Trail of Tears."

When the Civil War broke out, Tennessee was divided over whether to secede (withdraw) from the Union or to remain a part of the United States. It finally became the last state to join the Confederacy in 1861. From that time on, Tennessee was a battleground. Military forces moved into the eastern part of the state and occupied it for a good part of the war. Union general Ulysses S. Grant moved his troops along the Tennessee River to Pittsburg Landing in 1862, and it was there that the Battle of Shiloh was fought—a key battle of the war, won by the Union. Western Tennessee was now in the hands of the Federal Government. Grant attacked the Confederate Army's position around Chattanooga in 1863, and on the first day of the battle, General Joseph Hooker defeated the Southerners on Lookout Mountain. Two days later Chattanooga fell to the Union. In 1864 General George H. Thomas defeated Confederate General John B. Hood's troops in the Battle of Nashville.

Union General Joseph Hooker aided in the defense of Washington, D.C. at the beginning of the Civil War. He then fought in the battles of Bristoe Station, Manassas, Chantilly, and Williamsburg, where he earned the nickname "Fighting Joe." He continued to distinguish himself as a corps commander at Chattanooga but, when he failed to be named commander of the Army of Tennessee, he resigned from active duty.

George Henry Thomas, the Union general who commanded the Army of the Cumberland during the Civil War, was the only general to prevent his men from fleeing during the Battle of Chickamauga in September 1863. His brave action saved his army and gained him the nickname "Rock of Chickamauga." In 1864, he defeated the Confederate forces of John B. Hood in the fierce battles of the Franklin-Nashville campaign. Thomas's victories earned him a promotion to major general, the post at which he remained until his retirement in 1870.

Tennessee Senator Andrew Johnson, the only southerner who remained in the senate after his state seceded, became Abraham Lincoln's vice-president in 1865, and assumed the presidency after Lincoln was assassinated. Johnson called for the readmission of Tennessee to the Union, but was temporarily blocked by the many Congressmen who were determined to punish the South for the Civil War. Nevertheless, in 1866 Tennessee became the first Confederate state to be readmitted.

After the Civil War, Tennessee faced a long recovery process. Much of it was in ruin, and thousands of people were homeless. Many of the state's men had been killed in battle. In the central and western parts of Tennessee, many of the large plantations were broken up into small farms, and it took nearly 40 years for these farms to recover from the war. In the meantime, however, mining and manufacturing began to stimulate the economy. Then came the yellow fever epidemic of 1878, which killed almost two-thirds of the residents of Memphis, and greatly slowed the state's economic recovery.

After the turn of the 20th century, Tennessee gradually changed from an agricultural to an industrial economy. Highways and railroads were built. By the time of the Great Depression of the 1930s, manufacturing had almost overtaken farming as the state's leading economic force. The Federal Government's Tennessee Valley Authority helped the state create new jobs by taming the destructive, flood-prone Tennessee River, which increased the productivity of the area's farmland and generated vast amounts of electrical power. For these reasons Tennessee was not as severely affected by the Depression as were its neighboring states.

Tennessee became a leader in nuclear energy in 1942, when the Federal Government built one of the nation's first atomic energy plants at Oak Ridge. Because of the inexpensive sources of electricity and the natural resources in the state, new industries came to Tennessee after World War II. About 1,500 new plants opened between 1953 and 1963.

Tennessee's history since the Civil War has been one of growth. It is now industrial instead of agricultural. But despite all the changes, much of the old Tennessee still endures. A great deal of the wilderness that the early pioneers found is still there, and conservationists intend to keep it that way.

# Education

Education is one of the great advantages that Tennesseans offer their youth. The first school was opened in 1780, and today there are 140 public school systems serving approximately 850,000 students. About 200,000 students are enrolled in vocational education programs. There are over 30 institutions of higher education in the state including six state universities, ten community colleges, and private schools such as George Peabody College for Teachers and Vanderbilt University, both located in Nashville.

Julian Bond began his civil rights activities while a student at Morehouse College in Atlanta, taking a leading role in the Student Nonviolent Coordinating Committee (SNCC). Eventually he won a seat in the Georgia state legislature.

# The People

More than 60 percent of the people of Tennessee live in urban areas, and almost half of them live in the metropolitan areas of Memphis, Knoxville, Nashville, and Chattanooga. Most people in the state are American-born, and many of them are from British, Scotch-Irish, French Huguenot, or German stock. The Baptist church has the largest membership in the state, followed by the Church of Christ, the Methodists, the Presbyterians, and the Church of the Nazarene.

**Famous People**

Many famous people were born in the state of Tennessee. Here are a few:

**Roy Acuff** b.1903, Maynardville. Country-and-western singer

**Julius Ochs Adler** 1892-1955, Chattanooga. Executive of *The Chattanooga Times* and *The New York Times*

**Chet Atkins** b.1924, Luttrell. Country-and-western singer

**Frank M. Andrews** 1884-1943, Nashville. World War II Air Force general

**Jimmy Blanton** 1921-1942, Chattanooga. Jazz bass player

**Julian Bond** b.1940, Nashville. Politician, poet, and TV commentator

**James Brown** b.1928, Pulaski. Soul singer

**Hattie Caraway** 1878-1950, near Bakerville. The first woman elected to the United States Senate

**Davy Crockett** 1786-1836, Greene County. Frontiersman and hero of the Alamo

**John Cullum** b.1930, Knoxville. Actor: *Shenandoah*

**David Farragut** 1801-1870, Knoxville. Union admiral

**Lester Flatt** 1914-1979, Overton County. Country-and-western singer

**Ernie Ford** b.1919, Bristol. Country singer

**Nathan Bedford Forrest** 1821-1877, Bedford County. Confederate cavalry commander

**Abe Fortas** 1910-1982, Memphis. Supreme Court justice

**Aretha Franklin** b.1942, Memphis. Rhythm-and-blues singer

**Elizabeth H. Gilmer** 1870-1951, Montgomery County. Columnist who wrote advice to the lovelorn under the byline "Dorothy Dix"

**George Hamilton** b.1939, Memphis. Film actor: *Act One, Love at First Bite*

**Cordell Hull** 1871-1955, Overton County. Secretary of state under Franklin D. Roosevelt

**Randall Jarrell** 1914-1965, Nashville. Novelist and poet: *Pictures from an Institution, The Lost World*

**Ed "Too Tall" Jones** b.1951, Jackson. Football player

**Bill Madlock** b.1951, Memphis. Baseball player

**Dolly Parton** b.1946, Sevierville. Country-and-western singer

**Minnie Pearl** b. 1912, Centerville. Country singer and comedienne

**John Crowe Ransom** 1888-1974, Pulaski. Poet and critic: *Chills and Fever, Two Gentlemen in Bonds*

**Grantland Rice** 1880-1954, Murfreesboro. Sports columnist

**Oscar Robertson** b.1938, Charlotte. Hall of Fame basketball player

**Wilma Rudolph** b.1940-1994, St. Bethlehem. Three-time Olympic gold medal-winning runner

**Sequoyah** 1770-1843, Taskigi. Created the Cherokee alphabet

**Cybill Shepherd** b.1950, Memphis. Film and television actress: *The Last Picture Show, Moonlighting*

**Dinah Shore** b.1917, Winchester. Pop singer and TV hostess

**Bessie Smith** 1894-1937, Chattanooga. Blues singer

**Lynn Swann** b.1952, Alcoa. Football player

**Mary Church Terrell** 1863-1954, Memphis. Civil rights leader

**Tina Turner** b.1939, Nutbush. Rock and soul singer

**Alvin York** 1887-1964, Pall Mall. Congressional Medal of Honor-winning hero of World War I

### Colleges and Universities

There are many colleges and universities in Tennessee. Here are the more prominent, with their locations, dates of founding, and enrollments.

*Austin Peay State University,* Clarksville, 1927, 7,670

*Belmont College,* Nashville, 1951, 2,866

*Carson-Newman College,* Jefferson City, 1851, 2,022

*Christian Brothers College,* Memphis, 1871, 1,736

*David Lipscomb University,* Nashville, 1891, 2,272

*East Tennessee State University,* Johnson City, 1911, 12,055

*Fisk University,* Nashville, 1866, 774

*Knoxville College,* Knoxville, 1863, 1,306

*Lambuth College,* Jackson, 1843, 1,153

*LeMoyne-Owen College,* Memphis, 1862, 1,200

*Lincoln Memorial University,* Harrogate, 1897, 1,860

*Maryville College,* Maryville, 1819, 787

*Memphis State University,* Memphis, 1912, 20,578

*Middle Tennessee State University,* Murfreesboro, 1911, 16,780

*Rhodes College,* Memphis, 1848, 1,414

*Tennessee State University,* Nashville, 1912, 7,591

*Tennessee Technological University,* Cookeville, 1915, 8,244

*Tennessee Temple University,* Chattanooga, 1946, 1,400

*Union University,* Jackson, 1823, 2,009

*University of Tennessee: at Chattanooga,* 1886, 8,147; *at Knoxville,* 1794, 25,998; *at Martin,* 1927, 5,660; *at Memphis,* 1911, 2,001

*University of the South,* Sewanee, 1857, 1,171

*Vanderbilt University,* Nashville, 1873, 9,724

### Where To Get More Information

Department of Tourist Development
P.O. Box 23170
Nashville, TN 37202

# Further Reading

## General

Aylesworth, Thomas G., and Virginia L. Aylesworth. *State Reports: The Southeast: Georgia, Kentucky, Tennessee.* New York: Chelsea House, 1991.

## Georgia

Bonner, James C., and Lucien E. Roberts. *Georgia History and Government.* Spartansburg: Reprint Company, 1974.

Carpenter, Allan. *Georgia,* rev. ed. Chicago: Childrens Press, 1979.

Fradin, Dennis B. *From Sea to Shining Sea: Georgia.* Chicago: Childrens Press, 1991.

Kent, Zachary A. *America the Beautiful: Georgia.* Chicago: Childrens Press, 1988.

Martin, Harold H. *Georgia: A Bicentennial History.* New York, Norton, 1977.

Vaughn, Harold C. *The Colony of Georgia.* New York: Franklin Watts, 1975.

## Kentucky

Channing, Steven A. *Kentucky: A Bicentennial History.* New York: Norton, 1977.

Clark, Thomas D. *History of Kentucky,* rev. ed. Lexington: John Bradford Press, 1977.

Coleman, J. Winston, Jr. *Kentucky: A Pictorial History,* 2nd ed. Lexington: University Press of Kentucky, 1972.

Fradin, Dennis B. *From Sea to Shining Sea: Kentucky.* Chicago: Childrens Press, 1993.

McNair, Sylvia. *America the Beautiful: Kentucky.* Chicago: Childrens Press, 1988.

## Tennessee

Bailey, Bernadine. *Picture Book of Tennessee,* rev. ed. Chicago: Whitman, 1974.

Bergeron, Paul H. *Paths of the Past: Tennessee, 1770-1970.* Knoxville: University of Tennessee Press, 1979.

Carpenter, Allan. *Tennessee,* rev. ed. Chicago: Childrens Press, 1979.

Corlew, Robert E. *Tennessee: A Short History,* 2nd ed. Knoxville: University of Tennessee Press, 1981.

Dykeman, Wilma. *Tennessee: A Bicentennial History.* New York: Norton, 1975.

Dykeman, Wilma. *Tennessee, A History.* New York: Norton, 1984.

Folmsbee, Stanley J., et al. *History of Tennessee,* 4 vols. New York: Lewis Publishing Company, 1960.

McNair, Sylvia. *America the Beautiful: Tennessee.* Chicago: Childrens Press, 1990.

*Numbers in italics refer to illustrations*

# Photo Credits

AP/Wide World Photos: pp. 30, 31, 60, 61, 62, 91; Courtesy of Federal Express Corporation, all rights reserved: p. 70; Courtesy of Georgia Department of Industry & Trade/Tourism Division: pp. 3 (top), 7, 8-9, 12, 13, 15, 16, 18, 19, 20, 21, 22, 24, 26, 28, 29; Courtesy of Georgia Secretary of State: p. 5; Courtesy of Kentucky Department of Travel Development: pp. 3 (bottom), 33, 34, 36-37, 39, 40, 41, 42, 43, 44, 45, 46, 47, 48, 49, 50-51, 53, 54; Library of Congress: p. 27 (bottom); Courtesy of Memphis Visitor and Convention Bureau: pp. 71, 73; Museum of the American Indian: p. 85; National Portrait Gallery, Smithsonian Institution: pp. 27 (top), 52, 55, 56, 59, 86, 89, 90; New York Public Library/Stokes Collection: p. 88; Courtesy of Tennessee Office of Travel and Tourism: pp. 4, 63, 64, 65, 66-67, 69, 72, 74, 75, 76, 77, 78, 79, 80, 81, 82-83, 87.
Cover photos courtesy of Georgia Office of Travel and Tourism; Kentucky Department of Travel Development; and Tennessee Office of Travel & Tourism.

COBMAN SQUARE